Step by Step Guide

HOW TO BUY A HOUSE WITH NO BANK LOAN

By Dean Harris

Realtor, Investor, Author,
Licensed Mortgage Loan Originator
CA BRE License No. 01385246
NMLS License No. 973170

"It is your Attitude at the beginning of a task that determines Success or Failure."

- Corrine Dewlow

How to Buy a House With No Bank Loan

Table of Contents

Preface

That's great! You're going to buy a house. Among many other benefits, buying a house using this book can help you…

- get the house you want without a bank loan.
- avoid waiting months or years before you buy.
- buy at a discount without fees that banks charge.
- benefit from terms you didn't know existed.
- stop thinking that bad credit is a roadblock.
- teach even knowledgeable sellers about this.
- convince critics that this process succeeds.

Maybe you picked up this book because you know that owning at least one decent house represents more security than most any other investment. Not even the staff at the Stock Exchange could disagree.

Owning real property is also the foundation of wealth. Houses have made solid investments for centuries. Whether or not you care that owning your home is a smart investment, you know that everyone needs a place to live. With this book, you will have the opportunity to own your "place to live," not just because you need a house, but because it can also be a house you want.

There is at least one of five more reasons you will want to continue reading.

1 - You applied to the bank and they rejected you, or you expect to be rejected for a home loan.

2 - You want to be able to help yourself, or someone close to you, learn how to buy a house without a bank loan.

3 - You do not have the cash to pay for a house in full, days or weeks after submitting an accepted offer to the seller.

4 - You have the cash to pay the seller's entire asking price, but you do not want to part with your money that would be used as payment in full within days or weeks of making the seller an offer.

5 - You are curious and want to learn something about this interesting process.

It took decades until most smokers realized smoking was not good for their health. Then it took many years before people began accepting studies that showed soft drink consumers should stop drinking soda.

In contrast, there are few warnings about the hazards to your financial health when dealing with bank or other institutional home loans. There should be warnings, but banks don't want to even mention excellent home buyer and seller alternatives like the ones described in this book. Banks want to keep books like this from becoming popular. The reason is clear. The more people use this book's methods, the lower the bank profits.

In the years to come, more people will realize that doing deals without the bank is the better alternative. In spite of bank efforts to keep it secret, the process will continue to become better known and improve.

Our Family Secret

Why did my father choose to live in that country and buy a house there? Andorra is one of the world's smallest countries. Situated in the middle of the border between France and Spain, Andorra is a little-known tax haven landlocked high in the mountains of the Pyrenees.

He was raised in Athens Greece before spending most of his adult life in America. While working more than 40 years in New York City, he bought and sold several houses and commercial properties in the five boroughs. Many of his transactions did not involve bank loans.

Buying houses without bank loans helped him maximize the returns on his investments. In fact, he did so well that he was able to retire to Greece, but he still wanted more.

So why did he choose Andorra? Because he loved Athens but complained that it was too hot in the summer. He searched and found Andorra, a place to safeguard his money and a place where he could stay cool in the summer. But it was too cold in the winter. So every spring during his retirement of 28 years, he made the trip to Andorra and then returned to Greece every autumn.

Maybe your goal does not include an upscale retirement abroad. Since you intend to buy at least one house, why not make the purchase as smart as you possibly can? By the time you retire, your plans could exceed your dreams.

Make Payments but Not Mortgage Payments

This book will not refer to the commonly abused word "mortgage" when talking specifically about the debt owed on the house. In this book, you will only see "home loan" or the Promissory Note ("the Note") which is the correct term for the document describing the total borrowed debt owed on a house.

A mortgage is never repaid because the mortgage document's function is limited to officially offering the lender the physical house as collateral for the loan, but only if the borrower stops paying the Note.

The mortgage is nothing more than evidence that the lender, such as a bank, has the legal authority to foreclose on the house. In contrast, the Note is the physical document that is the home loan. The mortgage is not the home loan. The mortgage never needs to be "paid."

The abuse of the word mortgage does not end there. Here in the 21st century, genuine mortgages that offer the home as collateral are disappearing at a faster rate than ever. Now, the trust deed, also known as the deed of trust, is being mistakenly referred to as a mortgage. This book will not make that mistake either.

While the trust deed is also a document that is limited to offering the home as collateral for the Note, the mortgage document is only used in areas that enforce foreclosure through the judicial court process. Those judicial areas continue to shrink because the court system has become even less efficient following the overwhelming number of foreclosures after 2006.

The abuse of the word doesn't end there either. The government's SAFE Act created new laws regulating certain aspects of home loans. The new laws included a licensing system that covers real estate practitioners formerly referred to as "Loan Officers."

Sadly, the SAFE Act laws gave Loan Officers a less accurate formal title. Instead of "Loan Officer," the individual is now known as an MLO, or Mortgage Loan Originator.

Finally, an ARM should not be called an Adjustable Rate Mortgage. It's not a mortgage – it's a loan.

No wonder so many people are so confused!

To review: Only judicial areas use a mortgage to secure the repayment of the Note. Mortgages require that the court be involved if there is a foreclosure. Non-judicial areas use trust deeds for a less formal and more efficient foreclosure process.

(See Appendix D for "mortgage" versus "trust deed" and Appendix B for more about these two documents)

Introduction

The Difficult Truth

The following statement should not surprise you. Banks currently control the vast majority of home loans. It seems as though banks have always controlled home loans.

For generations we have been trained to believe that if we were not approved for a home loan by a bank or other institutional lender, we had to put our plans to buy a house on hold for an undetermined number of years or give up the idea of ever owning a home.

Are you sitting down? Good. The need for bank involvement is actually an illusion created by . . . banks. The reality is that banks are an unnecessary middleman. Banks bring their own unnecessary home loan expenses as well as additional expenses from their associated home loan middlemen.

In the past several decades, tens of thousands of smart home buyers and sellers have realized this truth and closed their own transactions. They used a step by step process like the steps recommended in this book.

Banks have wanted this kept secret because those home buyers used no bank or other institutional lender. That's one reason why so many still believe it is not possible to buy a house when no bank will approve their home loan. Why else do people still believe banks need to be the source of their home loan?

Much of the answer lies in the past few centuries.

Section A - U.S. History Affects You Today

How the History of Home Loans Affects You

At some points during the past several hundred years, banks had no significant role in home finance.

Occasionally throughout history, there have been intelligent, highly respected leaders who knew that banks should not have the power they possess. There was particular concern about the abusive role banks played in real property finance.

At times, some of those leaders succeeded in keeping banks from controlling our lives. So who were these leaders and how did they predict so many decades ago the problems we would be having with banks today?

Although today's international headlines involve even more dismal financial implications, it may surprise you that several founding fathers of the United States were adamantly against banks. James Madison and Andrew Jackson were two patriots who took the lead from Thomas Jefferson.

To quote Jefferson in 1802,

"If the American people ever allow private banks to control the issue of their currency, first by inflation, then by deflation, the banks and corporations that will

2

grow up around them will deprive the people of all property until their children wake up homeless on the continent their Fathers conquered.

I believe that banking institutions are more dangerous to our liberties than standing armies. The issuing power should be taken from the banks and restored to the people, to whom it properly belongs."

There were two events that prompted Jefferson and his fellow patriots to become so critical of banks.

The primary event had taken place many years earlier in England. The new American patriots had seen the severe damage done to the freedom of the people of Great Britain after the English allowed the creation of a banking system in the late 1600s that featured an independent and private central bank. This bank pretended to be a government institution. In reality, it was a closely held private business created by greedy men charging interest to issue currency and to create and manage various types of loans.

In 1694 the English dubbed their new central bank "The Bank of England." And it still exists today! This was the same bank that eventually caused the financial oppression of emerging America - the same banking system that essentially triggered the American Revolution. It also contributed to the reason for Jefferson's warning. America had wanted independence from England in order to avoid those kinds of mistakes.

What was the second event that prompted Jefferson's warning? The individual early American colonies had been experiencing

3

trouble establishing and agreeing on currency standards. In response, the First Bank of the United States had been launched in 1791. During its brief existence, the bank was under attack for having created more problems than it solved. Because of the widespread criticism, the First Bank of the U.S. was unable to have its 20 year charter renewed. It was closed in 1811.

Just a few years after First Bank of the United States closed, the colonies were again experiencing financial disagreements. In spite of Jefferson's warning to the new United States, a second American controlling central bank was established in 1816. Ultimately and for similar reasons, that bank was also unable to renew its 20 year charter.

In 1836, near the end of his second term as President, Andrew Jackson repealed the law that created the bank, ending its existence along with any plans for a future central bank. On his death bed years later, former President Jackson was asked what he considered to be the greatest accomplishment of his life. He answered, *"I killed the bank!"*

After 77 years with no central bank, the Federal Reserve, as it deceitfully came to be known, was created in 1913. In spite of its name, the Federal Reserve Bank was not, and never has been, a U.S. government institution.

The Federal Reserve could not have been launched without the enthusiastic and self-serving support of wealthy banker J. P. Morgan who was seeking to secure more money and power for him and his fellow greedy bankers.

This private institution has been profitably gaining control of many aspects of U.S. government policy steadily over the years.

4

Domestic housing is just one aspect of government policy that the Federal Reserve Bank influences to this day. Jefferson and Jackson would be very sad indeed.

The only other president to ever stand up to "The Fed" was John F. Kennedy. In June of 1963, he issued Executive Order 11110, which effectively abolished the Federal Reserve and gave monetary authority back to the government.

With this order, Kennedy directed the Treasury to print billions of dollars bearing the title "Silver Certificate." Kennedy's intentions were clear. The concept was simple yet strategically brilliant, the hallmark of many of his strategies.

These bills were to be strictly represented by, and limited to, the U.S. supply of silver. There was to be no interest charged for these new dollars. He wanted to help ensure that the government alone would be responsible for controlling the budget – not greedy bankers seeking profit at the citizens' expense. Kennedy sensed that his plan would avoid the danger that Jefferson predicted would be the result of bank inflicted excessive individual and national debt.

Immediately after Kennedy was assassinated, President Johnson directed the Treasury to destroy all existing Silver Certificate bills. Johnson was obligated to restore bank jobs to colleagues.

The Federal Reserve Bank's power to issue currency, for which the Fed had always charged interest, was reinstated despite the warnings of history and intelligent leaders. Especially with the benefit of hindsight, more and more people agree that a threat like the power given to the Federal Reserve Bank should be given back to the people, as President Kennedy tried to do before he was assassinated.

This little book is not intended as a call to radically alter or dismantle the banking system. While this book, by its nature, is critical, it exists to help you by teaching an alternative that works effectively within the system.

These pages make a sometimes complex subject relatively simple. It's a proven multi-step process that hopeful home buyers and sellers have used and should continue to use, that also directs home loan power away from banks.

Whether or not any banking reforms occur as a by-product, this book will create a better life for each of the buyers who follow its steps. Sellers can certainly benefit from it as well. For now, this book should be your secret – a secret golden door key.

While we are on the subject of history, this section would not be complete without talking about the housing struggles in every decade since the 1970s.

September 11, 2001 caused far more financial damage that certainly wasn't limited to housing, so that year is not included. However, that decade did not escape a most severe downturn.

There were some difficult years prior to the 1970s, but this section of the book will start with that decade.

It's important to keep in mind, that, with all of these setbacks, very few investments have shown such an incredible ability to bounce back, usually beyond the highest previous values.

The Home Loan Crises of the 1970s, 1980s, 1990s and 2008

In 1978, the housing industry and bank lending problems began to take center stage. Bank home loan rates started their multi-year rise into double digits. In fact, by the early 1980s, bank rates had climbed so high that home loan approval most often could only be issued by the homeowners who had equity to lend directly to hopeful buyers. Home loan lending remained firmly in the hands of those sellers, and not the banks, for many years.

How and why did this happen?

The failed policies of President Carter and the Federal Reserve caused home loan interest rates to rise to a high of 18.45% in October 1981. In fact, buyers had to pay more than 2 points to get that rate! Home loan rates would not drop and stay below 10% until 1991 (see the Associated Press news article from 1982 in Figure 1 below). In the decade of the 1980s, most home buyers could no longer afford bank issued home loans. As a result, sellers could not easily find buyers.

> Home loan interest rates rose to a high of 18.45% in October 1981.

Sellers had to offer their equity directly to the buyers in the form of a personal home loan in order to attract buyers. In effect, sellers had to become lenders or those sellers may never have been able to sell at all.

Section A - U.S. History Affects You Today

The government's failed policies had forced a return to Thomas Jefferson's vision of America. In the 1980s we became a country reliant on our own efforts and not dependent on banks for home loans. During that decade, hundreds of thousands of home buyers and sellers had benefited from seller carry backs.

As Jefferson had envisioned, our new self-reliance brought better results at far lower expense, though dark clouds were forming. This new test of the people's resolve was to be challenged in the 1990s.

Just like anyone who has been addicted to anything for an extended length of time, the addict is going to be tempted to return to the addiction when it is easier to indulge than to fight the urge to stay addicted. The bank home loan had been America's addiction for so long that it was difficult for home buyers to do without it. This was true for at least two reasons.

The Federal Reserve had a vested interest in overseeing a complete bank home loan recovery. The Fed made sure bank loans returned to single digits in the early 1990s. After stalling at rates over 14%, the Fed knew the drop to single digits would be as appealing as candy to a child.

What was the second reason for the decline of seller financing during the decade of the 1990s? Loans directly from sellers were still relatively new and experiencing growing pains. It was much easier to return to the familiar bank addiction than to have house shoppers struggle with "being clean" and choosing the seller as lender. Seller loans had become the better path for both home buyers and sellers.

8

Buyers and sellers can still choose the better path. Don't be tempted by low bank loan rates. Bank involvement is still riddled with excessive charges and time consuming procedural requirements, both from the bank itself and other related middlemen.

Consider it welcome news if you are rejected for a home loan from a bank. You will not only be able to buy a home with none of the well-known hassles from a bank but you will also be able to save lots of time, aggravation and money.

Government Lowers Ceiling On Home Loan Interest Rate

By SALLY JACOBSEN

WASHINGTON (AP) — The government is lowering its interest-rate ceiling on federally backed single-family home loans to 14 percent, the lowest rate since the spring of 1981, housing officials announced yesterday.

* * *

The decline from 15 percent to 14 percent goes into effect today on single-family home loans insured by the Federal Housing Administration, according to the Department of Housing and Urban Development.

The lower ceiling also will apply to single-family home loans guaranteed by the Veterans Administration.

It was the second drop in that rate in a little more than two weeks, and was part of a continuing trend in recent weeks toward lower interest rates. The first rate cut was one-half of a percentage point.

Donald Hovde, acting secretary of housing and urban development, called the decline "good news not only for the housing industry but for the many American families which have been kept out of the homebuying market."

He said the FHA rate was lowered "as a result of the continued strong downward trend in interest rates."

"While we are not out of the woods yet, we are headed in the right direction," he said in a statement announcing the new rate.

* * *

Mark Riedy, executive vice president of the Mortgage Bankers Association of America, said the reduction was "significant news" because 14 percent is considered by some a threshold level at which mortgage lending likely will pick up.

"I think it will have a very potent effect on the housing market," said Riedy. Mortgage bankers handle about 80 percent of the FHA- and VA-insured single-family home loans, he said.

Ceilings on interest rates for other FHA-insured loans also are being reduced by one percentage point over the next 10 days, the department said.

Starting today, the new allowable rates are 14 percent for both the level and graduated payment single-family mortgages, it said. The current 15 percent rate had gone into effect Aug. 9.

Private lenders had reported charging average interest rates of 17.22 percent for new mortgages in July, according to government surveys announced earlier this month.

Lenders are under no obligation to issue loans that carry interest rates at or below a government ceiling, but sometimes are willing to accept a lower return on such government-backed loans because they are sure of being repaid. If the ceiling falls too low, though, lenders simply refuse to make the loans.

* * *

The ceiling had risen to a record 17.5 percent in September. The rate last ran at 14 percent from March 9 through April 12, 1981, the department said.

The department said other new rates going into effect today are: 15 percent for permanent multi-family mortgages and 16 percent for interim multi-family construction and land development loans.

On Aug. 31, the following rate changes will go into effect: 17.5 percent for home improvement loans, 16.5 percent for mobile home loans, 16 percent for combination mobile home and lot loans, and 17.5 percent for historic preservation loans.

Figure 1 – Original Associated Press Article from November 1982

9

Section B - Handling Credit Problems

Solution for Credit Issues

Banks have strict guidelines about credit reports and scores that often disqualify buyers. Although credit scores are not as important in the type of transaction described in this book, you should be aware that sellers who intend to become lenders are advised to review the buyer's credit report and credit score. Sellers generally consider credit to be less significant than a bank would, but if your score is below 600, there is a chance you may scare some sellers away.

Why Has Credit Been a Problem?

It's no secret that credit has become tighter since the 2008 housing crisis. But what does the term "tight credit" really mean? Credit covers more than just the amount of the loan you qualify for. Credit also includes the minimum credit scores required by each lender. Tight credit means banks stop being as generous. Qualifying for a loan is more difficult. Tight credit almost always requires higher scores if bank loans are involved.

One cause of the housing crisis was the widespread abuse of consumer credit resulting in a mass reduction of credit scores.

Credit abuse continued for years. In 2015, Fair Isaac Co., the creator of the original FICO score, found that 78.5 percent of all consumers had scores that fell between 300 and 749. That was a dramatic score reduction from just a few years earlier. Since

Section B - Handling Credit Problems

FICO scores range from 300 to 850, that means only about one in five Americans would have a FICO score of 750 or higher.

Why is this credit score situation such a problem? A new home loan study shows that borrowers who had recently been approved for home loans from a bank had an average FICO score of 750 or higher. That has got to be discouraging to most of the 78.5 percent of the rest of consumers with lower scores, many of whom are hopeful home shoppers who must give up the idea of buying a house until their credit scores improve. For home shoppers, that could mean a wait of months or years.

You should not have to depend on a credit repair service that is too often a scam. The good news is that sellers who are willing to become your lender are almost always far less demanding than banks when it comes to your credit history. Although sellers are more likely to approve you with weaker credit, you may not want to risk scaring some sellers away. If you have a score at or below 600, it is worth getting help to improve your score. You can reduce your wait if you are careful about the credit firm you choose.

There are a few credit repair services that have developed a good reputation over the years. One of the more popular services is Heartland Credit Restoration.

Heartland's phone number is 888-573-2822. Their URL is: www.HeartlandCreditRestoration.com

It may be tempting to use your existing weak credit as another excuse to delay your home purchase. Remember that with the type of purchase this book endorses, many sellers do not consider weak credit a roadblock. Some sellers don't even look at the

11

credit reports, although sellers are generally advised to at least look at the buyer's scores.

If you are still concerned, or just interested in the subject of credit, next is advice about one type of credit. It has recently become a serious problem that weighs heavily against home buying. It is usually an obstacle that can be overcome.

Student Loan Debt

If you have one or more unpaid student loans, you may feel you are not qualified to buy a house. That assumption may very well be false.

The first thing you should do is get your current credit reports from all three bureaus at www.AnnualCreditReport.com - or from two bureaus at www.CreditKarma.com (see the additional references to credit as well as specifics about accessing credit reports and scores in Step 2).

Many who have student debt after attending only one college or university may be surprised to learn that the credit report shows more than one student loan – sometimes one for each semester. If that describes you, then get a student loan consolidation.

These student loans can and should be combined into a single loan. Showing only one student loan will improve your credit report, your score and your purchase chances, whether or not a bank will be the source of your home loan.

In any case, borrowers need to be making an effort to pay monthly. They should not use forbearance or other alternatives

12

that the government provides, allowing for postponement of the payments. Putting off the debt will usually result in paying more over the life of the loan. While we are on the subject of paying more, borrowers with private student loans that almost always have higher rates should work to pay them in full quickly or they should refinance at lower rates.

Know the Impact of Your Credit Score

When you understand the effect that specific FICO scores have on a bank home loan, you will be better prepared to negotiate the size of your monthly payment with a seller or an independent lender that isn't a bank or an institution.

The following chart will probably surprise you. It will give you a better idea about what kind of rate and monthly payment can be associated with a specific FICO score. The examples here will not be very different from the existing guidelines of institutional home loan lenders.

Keep this example in mind when negotiating with sellers.

While it is true that sellers will not be as concerned as banks about your credit score, you should show your score to the seller if it is above 680.

This is additional proof that your interest rate can and should be lower than whatever the seller first expects to charge you (see Step 6 - Negotiations)

Credit Score Impact
on a 30 Year Fixed Loan for $200,000

FICO Score	APR	Monthly Payment	Total Interest Paid
760-850	3.628%	$ 912	$ 128,479
700-759	3.850%	$ 938	$ 137.542
680-699	4.027%	$ 958	$ 144,861
660-679	4.241%	$ 983	$ 153,817
640-659	4.671%	$ 1,034	$ 172,165
620-639	5.217%	$ 1,100	$ 198,116

Figure 2 – How Credit Scores Affect the Cost of a Home Loan as of January 2016

Banks will be more demanding than most any other type of lender. Credit is just one of many reasons banks reject hopeful home buyers.

The following paragraphs identify more reasons you should be dealing directly with the seller for your loan.

14

Bank Requirements in Addition to Credit

Besides high credit scores, banks have been expecting borrowers to be able to offer higher down payments than in years past. You must fit the guidelines imposed by the bank, its investors and the government institutions that regulate banking activity. For instance, if your down payment is not 20 percent or more of the purchase price, you will generally have to pay mortgage insurance in the form of an additional monthly fee.

When the seller carries your loan, be aware that there should never be a demand for mortgage insurance.
Another common bank demand is also the cause for many loan rejections in recent years. Banks have been asking borrowers to show more income. In one example, banks will ask for more if the net income on your pay stubs is too low. Banks will want additional proof of higher income, but the proof must be in an acceptable form, such as business reports from a CPA or additional years of your most recent tax returns.

Another common bank demand expects that buyers reduce their debt levels. Banks will generally not approve a home loan if the borrower's debt level exceeds 42% of his or her income. It can be surprising how often hopeful home buyers don't realize how high their debt levels are (see Step 2 to help calculate your current debt level).

Credit and these other factors are the most common issues that make banks so difficult to deal with. They are just a few of the reasons you will be so much better off following the steps in this book and dealing with the seller directly.

Before Accepting an Approved Bank Loan

Jason Buyer made the mistake of choosing a 4.5% home loan from a bank rather than accepting an offer of a 5% loan directly from the homeowner. Jason had $8,000 as a down payment on a $150,000 house, which was acceptable for the bank loan as well as for the seller loan.

Jason's decision appeared to be smart. After all, he would be paying half a percent less with the bank loan and saving $43 a month. Was it smart? No.

More research would have shown him that, among other bank related expenses associated with the loan, he was expected to pay 2 points on his $142,000 bank loan, which is 2 percent of the loan amount, or $2,840. Loan origination charges added another $2,200 (see Appendix B – definition of Points)

Total bank related charges, including those points, came to $9,454. Add the down payment of $8,000 and Jason would have to pay the bank $17,454 before his house purchase closed and became official.

Compare that to $9,830 which was all he needed to close with the seller loan. The settlement charges on the 5% loan from the seller were under $2,000.

Because he decided on the bank loan, Jason will now have to choose between borrowing more (increasing the loan amount) or coming up with the extra cash at the closing table. He might have to do some of both. He may have to add more to his down payment. Without a higher down payment, he should expect more than 4 years of additional payments. Would the bank agree to a larger loan? Maybe.

Most sellers expect buyers to secure "conventional" financing so that they can receive the entire purchase amount at the closing table. Other sellers are smarter. They are not only willing, but prefer to be their buyer's lender.

These sellers know they can make tens of thousands more by lending, so they will be prepared to negotiate the price and terms. That is a big advantage, both for themselves and their buyers (refer to Figure 5)

To read and find out more about credit, see the additional references to credit as well as specifics about accessing credit reports and scores in Step 2.

Section C - Rent versus Own

This has been an ongoing debate for centuries. Aside from personal preference, there have been many months, years and even decades throughout history in which buying made more financial sense than renting.

The primary reason favoring the purchase has been appreciation over time. Other reasons include the ability to deduct home loan interest and property taxes. Homeowner's insurance can be deductible if you are running a small business out of your home. Home loan insurance can also be deductible but it is only a tax break in certain cases (see the inset near the end of this section for clarification)

Another critical factor that has often made buying the smarter choice is the fact that rent can be so high that it prevents the tenant's ability to save for a down payment. In fact, rent has been on a steady climb for decades, with a dramatically sharper increase since the housing bubble burst in 2008. With rental demand skyrocketing, landlords have felt comfortable raising rents to historical highs.

Deciding to become a tenant does have benefits. Tenants do not pay property taxes. They are not responsible for maintenance.

A tenant may decide not to buy because he or she thinks any money saved for a down payment should be used instead to invest in a mutual fund or stocks. Those investments are at much greater risk than they would be with a house purchase as an investment.

18

Tenants are often blind to the fact that stocks or funds could actually lose some or all of their invested cash. In addition to inevitable market downturns, there are usually ongoing fees, and they can be excessive.

For graphic comparisons of rent versus own since 1975, look at the chart in Figure 3 below. Also, the links after the chart provide more insight.

Figure 3 – Rent versus Own Monthly Payments 1975 to 2015

Notice in Figure 3 that the 2015 Home Payment Line is below the Rental Line and has been since 2010. That is an indication

Buy a House with No Bank Loan   Dean Harris

that buying is better than renting. You don't need a chart to tell you that buying is usually better, especially when you will be living in (or keeping) the property for five years or longer.

Historically, the median rent required 25% of the tenant's income, while the median loan payment required 22% of the homeowner's income. In 2014, the median rent required 28% of income, while homeowners needed only 20%. In many cases, the ratios favored homeowners even more dramatically.

These statistics will vary depending on location, home prices and rents, but the ratios won't usually vary by much. In order to satisfy the skeptics reading this section, specific locations and hard core dollar figures representing median income and home prices back up these statistics as seen at the following links:

quickfacts.census.com
www.neighborhoodscout.com

An excellent user-friendly yet powerful spreadsheet to interactively help you determine whether you should buy or rent is at the following URL:

www.kahnacademy.org/downloads/buyrent.xls

There are income tax deductions, such as loan interest and property taxes, which a house purchase gives you. Renting doesn't give you these financial breaks. Here is more information about the homeowner's insurance and home loan insurance tax deductions:

Homeowner's insurance that protects the buyer is different from home loan insurance that protects the lender.

In order for home loan insurance to be in force and be tax deductible, the loan must have been guaranteed by the Department of Veterans Affairs (VA), the Federal Housing Administration (FHA), the Government National Mortgage Association (GNMA) or the Rural Housing Service (RHS).

To qualify, the buyer would have to borrow more than 80% of the value of the property. This insurance is known as either PMI (Private Mortgage Insurance) or MIP (Mortgage Insurance Premium). They are almost always associated with a home loan from a bank.

Homeowner's insurance (not PMI or MIP home loan insurance) may also be tax deductible if a portion of the home is set aside for business use or the property is rented to a tenant.

The Home Loan Estimate

Next is a sneak peek inside at the initial home loan paperwork of a sample house purchase. Even if the estimate is prepared by a licensed Loan Originator, this document does not obligate you to accept the loan, whether the lender is a bank or a seller.

What are you paying in monthly rent? Chances are your monthly home loan payment will be less, especially after claiming the large home deductions that reduce your income tax obligations. As you know, you don't get these kinds of income tax breaks when you rent instead of own.

In this sample loan estimate, you won't see the critical tax breaks available that make buying so attractive.

Section C - Rent versus Own

Jason Buyer had been renting since he finished college. Although the choice he made with the bank home loan wasn't the better deal, buying a house was still a smart move. Owning had already proven to be better than renting for Jason, not just for financial reasons, but because it was the better lifestyle.

Michael Jones and Mary Stone are also going to buy a house. Like Jason's purchase, the house Michael and Mary want will cost $150,000. However, Michael and Mary will be borrowing directly from the seller.

The buyers will pay the monthly amount on line 19. But after their new home's deductions, their monthly payment will be closer to the amount on line 13.

Even if you have secured home loans in the past, the following descriptions of the items on this Loan Estimate will help you complete the paperwork for your upcoming home purchase.

Section C - Rent versus Own

1 Bernard Woods. Seller as Lender
4321 Random Boulevard · Somecity, ST 12340

Save this Loan Estimate to compare with your Closing Disclosure.

Loan Estimate

2	DATE ISSUED	2/27/2016	**6** LOAN TERM	30 years
3	APPLICANTS	Michael Jones and Mary Stone	**7** PURPOSE	Purchase
		123 Anywhere Street	**8** PRODUCT	Fixed Rate
		Anytown, ST 12345	**9** LOAN TYPE	☐ Conventional ☐FHA ☐VA ☒ Seller Finance
4	PROPERTY	456 Somewhere Avenue	**10** LOAN ID #	123456789
		Anytown, ST 12345	**11** RATE LOCK	☒ NO ☐ YES
5	SALE PRICE	$150,000		

Loan Terms

			Can this amount increase after closing?
12	Loan Amount	$142,000	NO
	Interest Rate	5.25%	NO
13	Monthly Principal & Interest	$784.13	NO
	See Projected Payments below for your Estimated Total Monthly Payment		

SAMPLE

			Does the loan have these features?
14	Prepayment Penalty		NO
15	Balloon Payment		YES $126,293 Due March 2023

Projected Payments

	Payment Calculation		Years 1-7	Year 8
16	Principal & Interest		$784.13	See Balloon Payment Above
17	Mortgage Insurance	+	0	
18	Estimated Escrow *Amount can increase over time*	+	206	
19	Estimated Total Monthly Payment		$990	

			This estimate includes	In escrow?
20	Estimated Taxes, Insurance & Assessments *Amount can increase over time*	$206 a month	☒ Property Taxes	YES
			☒ Homeowner's Insurance	YES
			☐ Other:	
			See Section G on page 2 for escrowed property costs. You must pay for other property costs separately.	

Costs at Closing

21	Estimated Closing Costs	$2,053	*See page 2 for details.*
22	Estimated Cash to Close	$9,053	Includes Closing Costs. *See Calculating Cash to Close on page 2 for details.*

LOAN ESTIMATE

PAGE 1 OF 3 · LOAN ID # 123456789

Figure 4 – Page 1 of 3 - Sample Loan Estimate (LE)

Section C - Rent versus Own

Closing Cost Details

Loan Costs			Other Costs		
23	**A. Origination Charges**	**$ 0**	**E. Taxes and Other Government Fees**	**$85**	**27**
	Points	$ 0	Recording Fees and Other Taxes	$85	
	Application Fee	$ 0			
	Underwriting Fee	$ 0	**F. Prepaids**	**$302**	**28**
			Homeowner's Insurance Premium (6 months)	$302	
24	**B. Services You Cannot Shop For**	**$455**	**G. Initial Escrow Payment at Closing**	**$74**	**29**
	Appraisal Fee	$405	Property Taxes $137.50 per month for 16 days	$74	
	Credit Report Fee	$30			
	Flood Determination Fee	$20	**H. Other**	**$ 0**	**30**
			I. TOTAL OTHER COSTS (E + F + G + H)	**$461**	**31**
25	**C. Services You Can Shop For**	**$1,137**	**J. TOTAL CLOSING COSTS**	**$2,053**	**32**
	Pest Inspection Fee	$100	D + I	$2,053	
	Title – Lender's Title Policy	$535	Lender Credits		
	Title – Settlement Agent Fee	$592			

SAMPLE

Calculating Cash to Close

Total Closing Costs (J)	$ 2,053	33
Closing Costs Financed (Paid from your Loan Amount)	$0	34
Down Payment/Funds from Borrower	$ 8,000	35
Deposit	– $ 1,000	36
Funds for Borrower	$0	37
Seller Credits	$0	38
Adjustments and Other Credits	$0	39
Estimated Cash to Close	**$ 9,053**	**40**

26   D. TOTAL LOAN COSTS (A + B + C) $1,592

LOAN ESTIMATE

Figure 4 – Page 2 of 3 - Sample Loan Estimate (LE)

Buy a House with No Bank Loan   Dean Harris

Section C - Rent versus Own

Additional Information About This Loan

41

LENDER	Bernard Woods		MORTGAGE BROKER	N / A
NMLS/__ LICENSE ID	N / A		NMLS/__ LICENSE ID	N / A
LOAN OFFICER	N / A		LOAN OFFICER	N / A
NMLS/__ LICENSE ID	N / A		NMLS/__ LICENSE ID	N / A
EMAIL	N / A		EMAIL	N / A
PHONE	N / A		PHONE	N / A

Comparisons

Use these measures to compare this loan with other loans.

42 **In 6 Years**
$58,126 Total you will have paid in principal, interest and loan costs.
$13,751 Principal you will have paid off.

43 **Annual Percentage Rate (APR)** 5.378% Your costs over the loan term expressed as a rate. This is not your interest rate.

44 **Total Interest Percentage (TIP)** 34.77% The total amount of interest that you will pay over the loan term as a percentage of your loan amount.

SAMPLE

Other Considerations

45 **Appraisal**
I may order an appraisal to determine the property's value and charge you for this appraisal. I will promptly give you a copy of any appraisal, even if our loan does not close. You can pay for an additional appraisal for your own use at your own cost.

46 **Assumption**
If you sell or transfer this property to another person, I
[x] will allow, under certain conditions, this person to assume this loan on the original terms.
[ ] will not allow assumption of this loan on the original terms.

47 **Homeowner's Insurance**
This loan requires homeowner's insurance on the property, which you may obtain from a company of your choice that I find acceptable.

48 **Late Payment**
If your payment is more than 21 days late, I will charge a late fee of $ 35.

49 **Refinance**
Refinancing this loan will depend on your future financial situation, the property value, and market conditions. You may not be able to refinance this loan.

50 **Servicing**
I intend
[ ] to service your loan. If so, you will make your payments to me.
[x] to transfer servicing of your loan.

Confirm Receipt

By signing, you are only confirming that you have received this form. You do not have to accept this loan because you have signed or received this form.

51

_____   _____   _____   _____
Applicant Signature   Date   Co-Applicant Signature   Date

LOAN ESTIMATE

PAGE 3 OF 3 · LOAN ID #123456789

Figure 4 – Page 3 of 3 - Sample Loan Estimate (LE)

Loan Estimate Field Descriptions

Page 1 of 3

1. At the top left, the seller's name is Bernard Woods. Mr. Woods will also be Michael and Mary's lender.

2. This sample estimate's issue date is February 27, 2016. This will not be the loan start date.

3. Michael and Mary currently rent at their address on Anywhere Street.

4. The house they want to buy is located on Somewhere Avenue in Anytown.

5. The purchase price is $150,000.

6. Even though this is a 7 year loan with a balloon payment, the term is 30 years. That reduces the monthly payment. So what's the bad news? Smaller monthly payments translate to a larger final payment.

7. The two basic loan purposes on the LE are "purchase" and "refinance."

8. The two basic LE loan products can either be "fixed rate" or "adjustable."

9. This is a "Seller Finance" purchase and had to be added to the blank line after the 3 other loan types.

10. The loan ID, which may be changed by the lender or the servicer when the home loan becomes active.

11. Since this is not a bank or institutional loan, it is not as likely to feature a rate lock, although that lock on the rate is still something that can be negotiated.

12. They will be putting $8,000 down, so Bernard Woods will be lending them $142,000 at 5.25%. Mr. Woods has agreed not to increase these amounts after the close.

13. Michael and Mary's monthly principal and interest payment will be $784.13.

14. Most sellers will want some kind of prepayment penalty. In this case, the buyers convinced Bernard not to include any such penalties.

15. This loan is based on a 30 year term, but the final (balloon) payment will be due 7 years later, in March 2024. That's when Michael and Mary expect to qualify for a refinance.

16. This repeats item number 13 above.

17. Seller financed transactions will not require mortgage insurance. Watch out for some sellers who may make this demand.

18. Michael and Mary should be able to deduct expenses from their monthly $206 escrow or impound account

27

that will automatically pay their property taxes and homeowner's insurance.

19. Their total (pre-tax) monthly payment will be $990. The after-tax total would be reduced by about $2,500 or more each year, simply by using the appropriate home deductions.

20. Michael and Mary agreed that their additional monthly payment of $206 will be paid from an escrow account. So their final monthly payment will actually be about $780, which is closer to their item # 13 payment above.

21. You are at the bottom of page 1 of 3, which is Costs at Closing. Refer to page 2, which is called Closing Cost Details. Page 2 itemizes the charges that, in this case, total $2,053.

22. "Estimated Cash (needed) to Close" will be $9,053. That represents the sum of the closing costs plus the down payment of $8,000 then reduced to $7,000 by the earnest money deposit of $1,000 previously paid to the seller. Again, refer to page 2 for details of each closing cost line item.

Loan Estimate Field Descriptions

Page 2 of 3 (Closing Cost Details)

23. A. "Loan Costs" – Origination charges, including points, application fee and underwriting fee are all

28

loan costs that are associated with a bank or institutional home loan. These charges are usually large amounts. None of them have any place in a seller financed loan.

24.   B. "Services You Cannot Shop For" – The buyer will pay for these outside vendors and no vendor is allowed to be chosen by the buyer. The agency that issued this form is trying to avoid loan abuse.

25.   C. "Services You Can Shop For" – This short list includes items that should not be skipped. You can choose those on the list and others.

26.   D. "Total Loan Costs" – This relatively small amount is typical for a seller financed sale. Although $1,592 is considerably lower than 2% of the purchase price, negotiations could reduce this even more.

27.   E. Other Costs – Government taxes and other fees will vary depending on the location of the house, but should not vary by much. Recording fees are nominal in almost all areas.

28.   F. Prepaids – (see Appendix B) In this case, six months of the homeowner's insurance needed to be deposited into the impound account upfront. This account, also known as an escrow account, should be created for all such sales to protect both buyer and seller.

29.   G. Initial Escrow Payment at Closing – Since this is not a future payment for property taxes, but instead covers past taxes owed until the loan closes, this cost is not a prepaid

item. This is known as a prorated item (see Appendix B for the definition of Prorations)

30. H. Other – When the lender is the bank, this section usually has many line items that the buyer is responsible to pay at the close. When the lender is also the seller, this section is usually empty.

31. I. Total Other Costs – Again, this relatively small amount is typical when a seller lends.

32. J. Total Closing Costs – Even when combining items D + I, these seller financed closing costs are nominal, which should be expected.

33. Calculating Cash to Close – Item J is the combination of item D and item I. Those items are added to these charges and credits:

34. Closing Costs Financed – Those expenses that the seller agreed could be "rolled into" the loan and paid monthly during the loan term. There are none in this transaction.

35. This is the down payment of $8,000 that seller and lender Bernard agreed to accept from buyers Michael Jones and Mary Stone.

36. Soon after the initial agreement between the parties, Michael and Mary posted a $1,000 Earnest Money deposit (see Appendix B for Earnest Money). That deposit appears again at the close as part of the down payment.

37. If it was agreed that any cash was to be paid to the borrowers at the close, that amount would appear here.

38. If the seller agreed to pay any lump sum at the close, usually intended to help the buyer close, that amount would appear here.

39. Any other lump sum debit or credit changes to the bottom line would appear here.

40. $9,053 is the full amount that Michael and Mary need to bring to the table in order to have their purchase close.

Loan Estimate Field Descriptions

Page 3 of 3 (Comparisons and Considerations)

41. The top of page three confirms the lender is the seller, Bernard Woods. He does not have (or need) an NMLS license. In fact, no licensed loan officer or mortgage broker is needed for this transaction.

42. Comparisons – In 6 Years, the total paid $58,126 will include principal, interest and fees. The total principal paid will be $13,751.

43. Comparisons – In a seller finance, the Annual Percentage Rate (APR) 5.379% is only slightly higher than the nominal rate. The nominal rate in this case is 5.25% (see Appendix B for "APR" definition).

44. The TIP represents the Total Interest Percentage paid for the entire loan. The TIP of 34.77% is relatively low because this is a seller financed sale. Many of these loan types feature a 5, 7 or 10 year balloon payment, which drastically reduces the loan's overall interest charge.

45. Bernard, the seller, gives notice here that he may order an appraisal that buyers Michael and Mary will need to pay for. The buyers should have firmly rejected the seller's request for a formal appraisal before this loan estimate was created.

46. Buyers Michael and Mary had seller Bernard agree to allow another buyer to assume their loan at any time during the 7 years. Bernard agreed, but with certain lender approved conditions. (see Appendix B for the definition of Assumed Loan, which can also be referred to as a Loan Assumption)

47. Homeowner's Insurance is important to purchase and to maintain payments (see Appendix A – Criticism # 5)

48. Late payment guidelines should be established before this Loan Estimate is created. In this case, Michael and Mary did negotiate a late payment rule for themselves that is more than fair. It would not be realistic to expect no penalty for a late payment. (see Step 6 – Negotiations)

49. A government required disclosure that seems obvious.

50. Certain third party services are recommended. Servicing seller financed loans by a skilled and objective third party firm is critical (see Appendix C–3rd Party Service Links)

51. Buyers Michael and Mary should sign and date this Loan Estimate without concern that this document commits them to the loan. This estimate is only intended to clarify loan terms. Their signature only means they acknowledge receipt of the Loan Estimate.

The three pages in Figure 4 (above) can be used as another tool to help you compare more than just the purchase price of a house with the cost of renting.

Moving Out of a Rental Unit

You may be thinking, "All of this seems like it could be great, but my lease doesn't expire anytime soon."

That may be the number one reason that renters decide to wait. Renters who make that decision rarely take action when the time is right. When the lease finally does come up for renewal, signing it is easier. The dream of owning usually dies.

Other reasons keeping renters in a rental situation, such as the closeness of family and friends, may be rationalizations. If they don't want to leave the area, there are almost always homes for sale in the same neighborhood as the rental they are living in.

The next section offers at least one solution among many suggestions if you feel like you are stuck in a lease.

How to Legally Break Your Lease

You may be saying to yourself, "If I could get out of my lease, I would use this book to learn how to buy a house, but I feel like I'm stuck. I don't want to break the lease because I believe I will have to pay the remaining months on my existing lease. I think it may not be worth having to pay the balance on my lease so I can buy a house."

If that describes you or someone you know, you should keep reading this section. It is possible to break the lease without owing the lease balance or having to pay penalties associated with leaving early.

In the unlikely situation that none of the following suggestions work, there have been purchases in which the former tenant was unable to break the lease but still found that paying the lease balance was the better strategy. The advantage of buying the house now was greater than the many disadvantages of staying in the rental unit.

Know Tenant Responsibilities under a Lease

With a standard lease, usually a landlord can't raise the rent or change other terms until the lease expires. This is true unless the lease itself allows for a change prior to the expiration of the existing lease, such as an added clause allowing the landlord to increase the rent after a set number of months.

A landlord is generally unable to force you to move out before the end of the lease unless you fail to pay the rent. You can also be evicted if you violate one or more important conditions of the

34

lease, such as hosting noisy parties on a regular basis or abusing the building's exterior or common areas.

If tenant violations occur, landlords in most states are still unable to take immediate action. They are required by law to follow specific procedures before they can end the tenancy.

For example, the landlord must give three days' notice to the tenant to pay the rent or leave before he or she can legally file a lawsuit which would only begin the eviction proceeding. The action to remove a tenant usually takes months before the eviction actually happens.

In contrast, the tenant must leave almost immediately if he or she has engaged in any illegal activity on the premises. The landlord has the right to post or deliver an "unconditional quit notice" that gives the tenant only three days to move out.

Four Situations that Allow You to Break Your Lease without Penalty

Most people know that tenants are legally bound to pay rent for the full length of the lease, which is typically one year, whether or not the tenant continues to live in the rental unit. Most people don't know that there are a few exceptions to that rule.

In the following situations, if you learn your rights, you may be able to legally move out before the end of the lease and not owe the remaining balance.

1. The Rental Unit Is Unsafe or Violates State Health Laws

If your landlord does not provide safe housing under local and state housing health and safety codes, a court would likely determine that you have been "constructively evicted." Therefore, you would have no further responsibility or legal obligation to pay the rent.

State laws set specific requirements for the procedures you must follow before moving out when the cause is a major repair problem that the landlord has delayed addressing or refuses to resolve. The problem must be serious, such as the lack of heat, electricity, pest infestation or a substantial mold issue.

2. You are on Active Military Duty

You have the right to break a lease, under federal law, if you enter active military service after having signed a lease. This is covered under the War and National Defense Service Members Civil Relief Act.

In order to qualify, you must be part of the "uniformed services," which includes the armed forces, commissioned corps of the National Oceanic and Atmospheric Administration (NOAA), commissioned corps of the Public Health Service, and the activated National Guard. You must give your landlord written notice of your intent to terminate your tenancy for those military reasons. Once the notice is mailed or delivered, your tenancy will terminate 30 days after the date that rent is next due, even if that date is months before your lease expires.

3. You Have Experienced Abuse

Some state laws provide early termination rights for tenants who are victims of domestic abuse, sexual violence or elder abuse, provided that specified conditions are met, such as the tenant having secured a restraining order.

4. Your Landlord Invades Your Privacy

In most states, your landlord must give you 24 hours' notice before entering your rental property. If your landlord repeatedly violates your right to privacy, or does things like removing window screens, turning off your utilities, or changing the locks, you would be considered "constructively evicted" as described above. This is usually enough to justify breaking the lease with no further payments.

Your Landlord and Finding a New Tenant

If you don't have a legal justification to break your lease, the good news is that you may still be off the hook for paying all the rent due for the remaining lease term. This is because, under the laws of most states, your landlord must make reasonable efforts to re-rent your unit—no matter what your reason for leaving—rather than charge you for the total remaining rent due under the lease. So you may not have to pay much, if any additional rent, if you break your lease. You need pay only the amount of rent the landlord loses because you moved out early. This is because state law generally requires landlords to take reasonable steps to keep their losses to a minimum—or, in legal terms, to "mitigate their damages."

So, if you break your lease and move out without legal justification, your landlord can't just wait until the end of the lease and then sue you for the total amount of lost rent. Your landlord must try to re-rent the property reasonably quickly and subtract the rent received from new tenants from the amount you owe. The landlord must not relax standards when seeking acceptable tenants. Also, the landlord is not required to rent the unit for less than fair market value, or to immediately turn his or her attention to renting your unit while disregarding other business. Your landlord can add legitimate expenses to your bill—for example, the costs of advertising the property.

If your landlord re-rents the property quickly (more likely in college towns and similar markets), all you will be responsible for is the (hopefully brief) amount of time the unit was vacant.

The bad news is that if the landlord tries to re-rent your unit, and can't find an acceptable tenant, you will be liable for paying rent for the remainder of your lease term. This could be a substantial amount of money if you leave several months before your lease ends. Your landlord will probably first use your security deposit to cover the amount you owe. But if your deposit is not sufficient, your landlord may try to collect the balance, immediately or soon after keeping your deposit.

What if it seems you have no legal termination method available to you?

Here's How You Can Still Break Your Lease Legally and Minimize Your Responsibility:

38

If you need to leave early and it appears you don't have legal justification to do so based on the above scenarios, there are better options than just moving out and hoping your landlord gets a new tenant quickly. You can limit the amount of money you will need to pay your landlord—and help ensure a good reference from the landlord. You know you will need to start looking for your next place to live, you need a good reference and you also know you will need to terminate your lease.

You can help the situation by providing as much notice as possible and writing a sincere letter to your landlord explaining why you need to leave. Ideally you can offer your landlord a qualified replacement tenant, someone with good credit and excellent references, to sign a new lease.

You could advertise but don't use craigslist.org. Free sites like craigslist.org have become a sanctuary for scammers who lie about themselves in order to grab the cash and run.

The same reason to avoid using craigslist.org is the reason to avoid interviewing a potential tenant. Scammers know how to ask questions that provoke illegal answers from you. Those answers often result in hefty court awarded fines. They can too easily turn themselves into victims, winning the right to collect based on violations of the Fair Housing Act.

In spite of any drawbacks, it is usually well worth the effort to get one of the above solutions to work for you. Is there a unique issue that applies to your situation? Try turning that issue into a qualified early termination.

Section D – 8 Ways to Buy a House

8 Ways to Buy a House without a Bank Loan

There are many who still believe that being rejected by a bank means your hope of buying a house is either dead or on hold.

In fact, there are at least a dozen ways to buy a house without needing a bank or other institutional home loan. This section will limit the list to 8 different ways. A few require only a small amount to begin to establish ownership of the house.

Here is the First Method

The first and most obvious method of buying a house without a bank loan involves paying a large amount of money. In fact, this method requires paying the entire purchase price in cash. Have no fear. Paying for a house in cash is not what this book is about.

These following paragraphs will provide descriptions of seven more methods that allow you to avoid having to depend on any bank or similar organization for a home loan. However, most of this book will focus on one preferred method that will put you (or your legal entity) on the deed as owner within 30 days of making your accepted offer.

After all, you will not, in fact, own the house until you (or your legal entity) is named on the deed. The hope of being named on the deed sometime in the future should not be acceptable to you as a home buyer anticipating full ownership. If you make the right choices, your wait should be no longer than 30 days.

40

Seven More Alternative Purchase Methods

The following strategies will also allow you to own a house without a bank loan. However, almost none of these strategies are recommended.

Some take too long to have your name or your controlling entity appear on the deed. Other strategies cannot be depended on to ever finally result in ownership. Then there are those alternatives that are not only undependable but will cost more effort and cash than they are worth.

We will begin with a method that is least likely to result in home ownership. That did not stop people from all over the world from trying this method. There are many who are attempting this right now. There will likely be even more in the future, in every corner of the earth and all walks of life.

2. Adverse Possession

In addition to paying cash in the amount of the purchase price, there is this lesser known method of buying a house without a bank loan. It is called Adverse Possession. Any house in which the owner of record has been absent, the house has been vacant and the property taxes have not been paid can become a target. Thousands of houses worldwide have been "purchased" at $10,000 or less in the last 30 years using Adverse Possession. If the hopeful "buyer" knows what to do, it could be easy.

Anyone who is aware of the property's situation can do a minor amount of additional research. They can then file the proper paperwork, pay the delinquent property taxes and for as long as

41

the original owner doesn't show up or pay the taxes, the "buyer" occupant can simply occupy the property.

If the owner never shows and the occupant has paid the property taxes for a specific number of years according to the laws in each area (U.S. States are listed in the link below) then those paid property taxes and a small fee also paid by the occupant become the occupant's purchase price. That occupant then becomes the legal owner. The entire process is usually between four and seven years.

In one specific case of adverse possession, the new owner had done everything required in the proper order according to the laws of the state. He had even recorded the final paperwork with the county which made him the legal owner beyond a shadow of a doubt. However, the bank that held the home loan identifying the previous owner as the borrower was determined to foreclose.

The bank's attempts were ill advised, since the collateral described on the mortgage was no longer owned by the bank's borrower. Therefore, the bank could not legally foreclose on the house and was forced to withdraw their legal action.

The Adverse Possession "purchase" method is valid in various countries of the world with some relatively minor differences.

Here is the link (active for decades and still valid as of February 2016) that describes the Adverse Possession laws for each state in the United States:

http://statelaws.findlaw.com/property-and-real-estate-laws/adverse-possession.html

3. Tax Lien Default

A tax lien that results in default is another method of becoming the owner of a house without a bank loan. It is only marginally more likely to result in home ownership than playing by the rules of Adverse Possession.

So what is a tax lien? How and when can the buyer of a tax lien see the lien result in home ownership?

When the current homeowner has not paid the property taxes, the owner will then owe the tax plus interest and penalties until the entire overdue tax bill is paid. A government authority will, at some point during a delinquency, place a tax lien on the property.

Tax lien "certificates" representing the unpaid amount then become available for purchase by almost anyone. The certificates are usually an excellent investment with typical returns between 7% and 50%. In his book, "The 16% Solution," Joel Moskowitz describes the process in detail with a focus on the 16% returns in the state of Arizona.

When the current homeowner finally does pay the overdue property taxes, the investor of the certificate receives that payment, including interest, fees and penalties directly from the property's tax office.

If, after a specific number of months or years, the current homeowner never pays the taxes, the lien actually becomes potentially much more valuable.

You, as certificate owner, can foreclose as if you were the only bank holding the only loan, even if one or more banks have existing loans on the property! The banks would lose. Their loans would be completely erased and most other liens would disappear as well. You would become the new owner free and clear after having paid nothing more than the property taxes and foreclosure expenses!

The reality is that, in most cases, the existing bank would likely step in and pay the overdue property taxes including interest and any penalties.

4. Lease Option

One of the best known techniques for buying a house without the bank is also the most popular. From a buyer's point of view, lease options are highly overrated for the reasons described below.

For those anxious buyers who can't wait until they qualify to buy a house using a bank loan, they can talk to the seller about leasing the property directly from the seller with an option to buy at a specific current price that will not change during the lease term, even if the property value increases. The term of the lease agreement usually lasts one to three years. No later than the end of the lease term, the buyer hopes to be able to buy, usually by qualifying at a bank.

One reason this method is not endorsed in this book is because you do not own the home during the term of the lease. As is the case with the majority of these alternative purchase methods, potentially your only benefit is that you have temporary use of the house.

Technically you are still leasing as any tenant would, except that you are paying more every month than most renters would pay for a similar property. Why are you paying more? The owner has given you the option to buy known as "First Right of Refusal." What does that mean for you?

During the term of the lease, the owner will not be able to accept any other purchase offers. By the end of the term, if you are still unable to buy the house, the owner can find another tenant, accept an existing purchase agreement or put the house up for sale. Many owners decide to offer another lease option to someone else.

Owners who keep offering lease options generally make far more than those who offer their house for rent or lease with no option to purchase.

The most disturbing statistic about a lease option almost always favors the owner of the house. It leaves the hopeful buyer who never does qualify with nothing to show for his or her one to three years of excessive monthly rent. The would-be buyer also suffers the loss of a hefty non-refundable deposit.

How often is the hopeful buyer left without the ability to purchase at the end of the lease term? Statistics compiled during the past 20 years show that 92% never do qualify for the purchase of the leased house. They did not qualify at any time during the lease option or on the day the option expired.

Is there any better news regarding a Lease Option? Yes. The buyer who is not sure of his or her capacity to complete the transaction might prefer a Lease Option to a Land Trust or a Land

Contract. At least when a buyer fails to qualify at the end of the term, the loss is limited to the purchase option and any amounts already paid.

In a Land Contract, failure leaves the buyer on the legal hook for the unpaid loan balance, which will usually result in a recorded judgment against the buyer and will seriously damage the buyer's credit.

5. The Land Trust

Although there is one serious drawback to this method for buyers, a Land Trust can be very beneficial in many ways to both the buyer and the seller. The seller sets up a Land Trust and becomes the Beneficiary of the Trust. Legal title is held by the Trustee, but the Beneficiary (seller) has full use of the property. The seller is even able to assign the use rights.

The Trustee is only allowed to perform one function – to foreclose if the buyer stops making payments. The Trustee can only begin the foreclosure process at the request of the Beneficiary. So the Trustee does have legal title, but it is known as "bare" legal title.

With a Land Trust, banks and insurance companies continue to view the original borrower is the owner. In fact, the seller still has title to the house; however, the seller's title is equitable title instead of legal title.

The Land Trust allows the seller to transfer the use of the property, and its equity, to you, the new buyer and borrower, by naming you as the holder of the "Beneficial Interest" in the property. Legal title does not get transferred to you, the buyer, until you have paid the Note in full. This is a serious drawback.

You and the seller close your deal, but this time the seller quietly transfers "beneficial interest" in the trust to you as the new "equitable" owner. It is quiet because there is no requirement to officially record the transfer of beneficial interest to any private or government agency.

Because Land Trusts convert real property to personal property, you receive a bill of sale naming you (or your legal entity) as the buyer. The only records of the event are the documents between the seller and you. The seller stays on as the Beneficiary. Loan payments and insurance can still have the seller's name on them.

You and the seller may arrange to make monthly payments to an account servicing firm. The servicer then pays the existing debts on behalf of the seller. This means the payment is coming from the original owner. The loan gets paid as usual and no suspicions are raised. That benefits both you and the seller.

In general, if the advantages of a Land Trust were better known, it would probably become at least as popular as a Lease Option. However, any legal document with the word "trust" in it ironically often generates fear.

The most obvious fears are fear of the unknown, a fear of cost and a fear of complexity. Be aware that you have the tools to create the Land Trust yourself without the services of an attorney, especially in this era of Nolo.com and Legal Zoom.com.

Keep in mind that a Land Contract is not a Land Trust nor is a Land Contract a trust, but a Land Contract is generally easier to create. Because it is easier and also offers its own benefits to the buyer and seller, the Land Contract has been the more popular choice, though not necessarily the better choice.

6. The Land Contract

A Land Contract, which can also be referred to as an "Installment Land Contract" (ILC) or a "Contract for Deed" (CFD) is another financing tool that does not require bank involvement. It also isn't required to be officially recorded, so it doesn't raise any suspicions. However, if you are the buyer, you would want the contract recorded to keep the seller honest.

What are the two biggest differences between a Land Trust and a Land Contract? The Land Contract does not offer the benefits of a revocable trust and it does not offer the benefits of converting real estate into personal property.

In a Land Contract, the buyer and seller agree to the terms of the sale in a private Note. The terms feature the seller's agreement to accept installment payments instead of receiving all of the equity at once.

Sellers should appreciate the tax benefit that installment payments provide. Instead of receiving the entire current market value (or asking price) of the property, the seller will only owe income tax on the sum of the monthly payments received each year minus the deductions. If the seller agrees to this, it may mean the seller prefers to avoid the involved process of a 1031 exchange, which is another method of avoiding capital gains taxes on the house sale. Sellers should be sure the land contract contains a forfeiture provision, under which a defaulting buyer may be evicted like a defaulting tenant.

Buyers have full use of the property which is similar to a rental, a Lease Option or a Land Trust. Sometimes full use of the property is all the hopeful buyer wants, as long as there is a chance of owning that property at some agreed upon point in the future (see Equitable Title vs. Legal Title in Appendix B). The Land Contract is not recommended in this book. Like the Land Trust, you do not get legal title until you have made all of the home loan payments in the contract.

7. Private Money and Hard Money

These two types of loans are additional methods of avoiding bank involvement. However, because they both come at a steep price, they are usually used prior to a bank loan as relatively short term loans that last from a couple of months to five years. They should not be confused with each other but many borrowers (and even some lenders) have a tendency to use the labels interchangeably.

The biggest difference between the two is that legitimate hard money lenders are licensed and regulated. Following the mortgage meltdown, there are far more rules, fines and watchdog agencies, forcing lenders, especially hard money lenders, to be more careful than they have ever been.

In contrast, private money sources are most often family, friends and referrals. When a private money deal is being negotiated, the transaction almost always takes place directly between the borrower and the lender without requiring lender licensing or adherence to any other organizational guidelines.

49

Both sources share some common traits. Their steep costs begin with higher than prevailing interest rates. Both usually feature large fees as well. Borrowers are generally more desperate when looking at these financing types.

Private money rarely advertises while hard money is actively promoting their lending as a business to attract clients. Since hard money sources are often private money lenders, those hard money lenders would need to charge higher fees in order to make a profit. Ironically, the hopeful buyers these types of loans attract have either been rejected or expect to be rejected for a home loan by banks.

Although none of the preceding methods are highly recommended by this book, each buyer and seller situation may call for one of those preceding methods to be used in spite of the method's faults.

Now it's time to introduce the one technique that offers the most bang for your house buying buck. You are about to find out why this method is more powerful than all the others, including paying entirely in cash.

The Best Way to Buy with No Bank Loan

8. Immediate Deed of Trust (IDT)

The IDT document, or its mortgage equivalent (see samples of both online at www.bankfreehouse.com) describes a much more unique and effective alternative to a bank loan.

Section D – 8 Ways to Buy a House

What makes it unique and powerful?

With an IDT, the buyer becomes the legal owner, usually less than 30 days after signing the agreement with the seller. Keep reading to find out the reason that one benefit, by itself, is so important. You will also want to know every IDT advantage.

The IDT is the focus of the rest of this book. It will be at the center of everything you will do to accomplish your goal of buying a house with no bank loan as efficiently as possible.

An IDT can be used in non-judicial areas in any one of 3 scenarios in which the seller is ready and willing to offer you the title to the house quickly. (In judicial areas, use a mortgage – see the sample seller finance mortgage online)

Briefly, here are the 3 scenarios describing each of the 3 seller situations. More detailed explanations follow in Section E.

The seller...

1. ...owns the house free and clear.

2. ...has a balance on one or more existing loans.

3. ...has a balance on one or more loans and the seller offers to lend the buyer all, or a portion of his or her equity as well.

Section E – Three Loan Types

3 Loan Types Included in the IDT

1. "True" Seller Financing

If the seller owns the house "free and clear" (meaning there is no outstanding home loan owed by the seller) then the loan that the seller offers you, the buyer, is known as one of the following: Pure, Straight or True Seller Financing.

2. "Subject To"

If the seller has an outstanding loan (usually one loan) and agrees to have the buyer take over the payments and the seller agrees to have his or her name remain on the pre-existing loan(s), this agreement is called "Subject To." The buyer agrees to pay "subject to" the terms of the existing loan or loans as well as other liens, if any.

So why won't recording the new trust deed with an additional "Subject To" clause raise red flags with the existing lender? If the bank remains unaware, it could be that the loan had been created by a huge bank, or it was serviced by MERS and sold to a collateralized pool. In those cases, there's an excellent chance that no one knows where the original Note is, or who holds it, so none of the methods that allow a lender to recognize the transfer are triggered.

Bank employees who may be aware of the identity of the original borrower are far removed from the people processing the payment. So as long as payments keep coming in, then no alarms are sounded.

3. AITD or Wrap

These are also called All Inclusive Trust Deed (AITD) or wraparound (a.k.a. wrap) financing. After the sale, the pre-existing loan or loans will remain in the seller's name as borrower. The original lender(s) must still be paid "subject to" the original loan terms and liens. This arrangement is different because it includes yet another loan in which the seller is the lender and not the borrower.

The new deed must be recorded, though the bank is not notified following the recording. As with the Subject To, the bank's discovery of ownership transfer is the responsibility of the bank.

If payments continue to be timely, the bank is unlikely to learn about the transfer and, almost certainly will not take collection action of any kind.

The Owner's Reasons for Selling

Why any of the 3 sellers would want to sell by offering to "carry" the Note depends on which of the three types of seller financing is offered.

If the seller is offering number 1 above (True Seller Financing), it usually means that the owner is financially comfortable. The seller may be a legal investment entity, having paid cash, or a lower price than the current sale price. The investment's goal is to create a relatively long term income stream. That stream would be far more profitable than most any other investment. (Refer to Figure 5)

53

The seller, if not an investor, is usually older and will have finally paid off the loan. The seller may also have inherited the house from older relatives.

In any of those cases, the seller's preference here is to receive periodic payments similar to an annuity. The seller may also want to avoid receipt of a lump sum that could trigger an excessive capital gains tax obligation. Sellers with 100% equity often already have another place to live or will not have much trouble quickly securing another place to live.

In a situation like number 2 above (Subject To), the seller is usually having financial difficulty of some kind. There may have been little or no interest from buyers at the price needed to sell. In any case, the seller has probably been unable to pay the home loan, resulting in one or more late payments or anticipate being late. In cases like this, the seller is usually desperate, which clearly gives you, as buyer, a big advantage when negotiating the terms of the sale.

In number 3 above (All Inclusive Trust Deed), the seller may or may not be having difficulties. By creating an AITD, the seller has the opportunity to generate monthly income in excess of the monthly payments to the existing lender. This can be a clever tax strategy, especially for those who do not want to be bound by the many rules of the IRS 1031 exchange.

It is time for you to begin using each of the steps to purchase your house.

Step 1 - Collect and Organize

GATHER AND ARRANGE ALL OF YOUR FINANCIAL PAPERWORK

"Organization is the first of the essential skills that leads to success." - Michael Faraday

As mentioned earlier, unless you have the entire purchase price in cash, you must not skip this step or any of the following steps. If you are already familiar with the home buying drill, you may be upset to see this step in a book that is not about the traditional home purchase. It is here for a reason.

The fact remains that before you even begin searching for any property where you will be using any type of financing, you will need to take a hard look at your existing finances. If you have completed the tasks as described in this step in the past 30 days, you can skip this step and move on to Step 2. You may have done these tasks in a previously unsuccessful attempt to secure a loan before buying this book. If that attempt was more than a month ago, continue with this step.

If your credit reports and scores in your possession are more than a month old, the first thing you should do is get your most recent credit reports from each of the three bureaus at www.AnnualCreditReport.com or from two bureaus at www.CreditKarma.com (get more info in Section B)

Step 1 - Collect and Organize

Get your financial paperwork together even if you think you know your finances well enough to write them all down from memory. No doubt you will have paper documents, even if you use Quicken or other record-keeping software.

Once you have the documents listed below, as well as the printed reports from your software, you will be able to more accurately compare your situation to the qualifying scenarios that follow in Step 2.

Do not let the list below intimidate you. At no point should you surrender to an inner voice that may try telling you this will be a waste of time.

Just go ahead and get it all together. The list is comprehensive but can vary a bit from the final list depending on lender demands and the unique details of your situation.

Here is a list of the documents you should gather:

- If you collect a paycheck, your W-2 forms from the previous two years

- If you own a business, the year-to-date Profit and Loss statements

- If you are paid a salary, the most recent 30 days of paycheck stubs

- Two years of your latest tax returns

- A complete list of your debts, such as credit cards, student loans, vehicle loans and child support payments.

- Include each debt's monthly payment and that debt's current balance

- A complete list of your assets, including the latest 3 months of bank statements, mutual fund statements and dividend statements

- Records of other assets, such as real estate deed(s), vehicle title(s) including child support and alimony payments, if applicable.

Once you have collected these documents and continue reading, you will begin to get a more solid idea of how much house you will be able to afford.

Keep in mind that it is difficult for anyone to truly be objective about their own finances. It is even more difficult if your paperwork is inaccurate, incomplete or missing. It may not be easy, but you will need this documentation and those printed software reports, whether or not a bank is ultimately the source of funds that approves your home loan.

By now you have collected and organized your documents and reports. If you haven't completed this task, you won't be able to make sense of the following section. Do not skip to Step 2 until you have finished this first step's chores of collecting, organizing and reviewing.

If you are concerned that this process already seems ordinary and too familiar, then you should know that each of the following steps will become more unique to this less traveled but highly rewarding purchase path.

Step 2 - Apply and Learn

FULLY UNDERSTAND THE RIGHT LOAN TERMS FOR YOU

"Tell me and I forget. Teach me and I remember. Involve me and I learn." - Benjamin Franklin

Take what you gathered and organized in Step 1 and use it to get fully "involved" in this Step so that you truly learn to make it work for you, even if what you gathered and organized is not impressive right now.

Unless you have already been declined in the past three months, or you have already decided not to accept an approved loan from a bank, you will be applying for a traditional bank home loan. Why?

You may be thinking, "I thought this book specifically shows you how to avoid banks?" Just keep in mind that you will benefit from learning how the bank thinks. Meeting with a banker will give you a better idea about which houses you should be looking at and which ones to avoid.

This book advises you about how to go ahead with your house purchase after a bank or other financial institution has made a decision. You do not have to accept the bank's decision even if it results in an approval. You may decide their fees are too high or their terms are unfair. That is often the case, so your rejection

58

of their approval would be a wise decision. Even if you don't use your approval, there may be a few sellers who want to know you were approved.

This book is not about assuming that banks will reject your application for a home loan. So, for a number of good reasons, it is important that you actually apply, whether or not you expect to be rejected.

You will be using the bank to help teach you more about this first phase of the purchase process – as it exists this month – not last month. Banks don't charge for this current and valuable one-on-one education in real estate finance. So you should not hesitate to take full advantage!

Which Realtors Will Provide the Most Value

At this point you may decide that you want or need help with the entire process before you go any further. Although everything is negotiable, the services of a Realtor are almost always free of charge to you as the buyer. That's because the seller traditionally pays their Realtor's commission and yours. You may consider the quality of the help to be more important than the fact that it's free. Yes, you can succeed simply by following the steps in this book, but that doesn't necessarily mean you should do so without qualified assistance.

What is the definition of "qualified" assistance?

Although it won't be easy, finding a Realtor who has experience with seller financing would be a very helpful element of your journey through the process. If you find one, then you would want to know if that experience was gained by representing the buyer or the seller. His or her experience may have included the buyer at one point and the seller in a different transaction. That combination of both buyer and seller experience would give you the most effective help.

This is not to say that an experienced Realtor with little or no background in seller financing would be useless. Realtors have access to information about sellers that goes further than just the data in the MLS. Much of the additional and often critical info they can get is not usually available to the public on the web.

Where to find the right Realtor? There are probably at least one or two names of Realtors you would recognize as having served your local area for the past few years. Their familiarity with your neighborhood usually covers relatively large areas, specific homes and many local individuals, whether or not those individuals had ever been that Realtor's clients.

Sometimes, the Realtor represents a brokerage that is known for assisting and promoting creative financing. They may have only participated in one or two of the eight creative methods described in Section D. But the Realtor who works for such a broker would probably also have invaluable connections to creative financing affiliates who specialize in seller financing. How many of the eight methods are they familiar with or have experience with? As with most questions, the best way to get answers is to call or visit the Realtor.

On the other hand, a Realtor with less than 5 years of overall experience would likely not be as much help. Chances are great that person is not familiar with creative financing, never worked with it and is probably not affiliated with any other professional who embraces the concept.

Whether or not you choose to use an experienced Realtor, you will do well to get additional help in order to most effectively communicate your wants and needs to any of the sellers you will be meeting with. Refer to Step 6 - Negotiations and Appendix C - Resources Guide in this book for a list of third party service and other resource links.

Here are some questions to ask the Realtor:

- Have you ever worked on transactions involving creative financing of any kind?

- Have you ever recommended seller financing as a benefit to any of the sellers whose homes you listed?

- Do you have experience representing buyers in their search for houses featuring sellers willing to lend?

- Why do you consider yourself an excellent negotiator?

- How many of your former clients can I contact?

- Are you also a Mortgage Loan Originator licensed by the NMLS?

- Can you recommend any other real estate and home loan professionals who work with seller financing?

Whether or not you use a Realtor, your credit report and score may be important. If a bank were reviewing your qualifications, the report would be critically important. If you have any questions about your credit; such as how and why your credit might affect this type of purchase, the next section should help.

Credit Score Concerns (see also Section B)

From 2008 through 2015, banks were steadily increasing their credit score requirements. Recently, in order to qualify for the lowest interest rates, your middle FICO score would have to be at least 720 out of a perfect 850. (Refer to the glossary for FICO and an explanation of middle FICO). By the way, the lowest possible FICO score is 300.

You should be happy to know that seller financed home purchases do not follow strict credit guidelines. Banks, on the other hand, are very strict about enforcing specific minimum scores for any of their home loan programs. Scores below the lowest minimum will result in a home loan rejection by the bank. This is not necessarily the case with a seller.

Your home loan application may only affect your credit score by indicating one new inquiry.

In contrast, you can get your one free annual credit report from each of the three credit bureaus without charges or penalties at www.annualcreditreport.com. This will not affect your credit scores. Neither does getting your credit report through a credit monitoring service, such as Experian's Triple Advantage, or getting your personal report directly from any bureau after you have experienced an adverse action, such as being declined for credit or if you are a victim of fraud.

Step 2 - Apply and Learn

For many people, one additional credit inquiry will not change their score at all. For others who know they already have 5 inquiries, they should be aware that 6 or more inquiries could result in a reduction in their score of 10 or more points. Have you checked your credit reports lately? Do you know what, if anything, affected your score?

You are allowed one free credit report every year from each of the three credit bureaus: Equifax, TransUnion and Experian. However, you can only access those free reports designated by law from one website: www.annualcreditreport.com.

Although the reports are free, your credit scores from this site for each bureau will NOT be free of charge. There are many useful utilities to check your credit scores. Watch out for hidden charges, even on annualcreditreport.com.

At the time of this writing, there is an outstanding and popular website that offers both the reports and the scores at no charge. CreditKarma.com is, however, limited to two of the three bureaus. The site offers information from both TransUnion and Equifax but not Experian. Two free scores is a bargain, especially when it costs nothing for those scores that give you a better idea about where you stand.

Remember, it is difficult to be objective about your own finances. So if you haven't already walked in, you should visit the bank's home loan department after you have thoroughly completed Step 1 above, then read and absorb the rest of the items here in Step 2.

Your Deposit and Down Payment

This subject kills more potential house purchases than lender rejections. It's a shame that so many hopeful buyers don't even begin Step 1 of the purchase process based on the often mistaken belief that they don't have enough of a down payment.

In the kind of transaction described in this book, many more terms are negotiable than those of the far less flexible bank home loan. The size of the deposit and down payment are two more items you need to discuss with the seller to find out what amounts would be mutually acceptable.

The next step; Step 6 – "Negotiation" will dive deeper into how you can successfully reduce a seller's deposit and down payment expectations. The basic argument a buyer should make is to remind the seller that a larger down payment increases the seller's immediate capital gains tax liability. Step 6 will go further by showing you how to combine related multiple terms and play them against each other.

Banks do offer "no down payment" home loans depending on which government agency guarantees the bank loan. The agencies that make this offer are the Veterans Administration (VA) and the U.S. Department of Agriculture (USDA). These offers come with restrictions. Many buyers find those agency guidelines and loan terms too restrictive, even if you qualify. If you were never a veteran of the armed forces or you are not buying a house in a very rural part of the country, neither program will be available to you anyway.

Does the FHA bank loan's traditional minimum required 3.5% down payment compare favorably to the terms of a seller financed down payment?

If you know that many applicants do not qualify for that low FHA loan down payment rate, and that you may be one of them, then the answer is yes.

One of the ways that borrowers can increase their bargaining ability as well as lower their monthly home loan payment is by increasing their down payment.

The most successful seller financed buyers offer a minimum of 10% down. Depending on the importance placed on other seller financed loan terms, buyers and sellers have traditionally agreed to a wide range of down payment sizes from zero to 50%.

You will get a better sense of how much of a down payment you should offer after reviewing Step 6 - Negotiations.

Your Income

What is important to banks will often not matter as much to sellers willing to lend. There are exceptions.

If your income is less than $50,000 a year and you want to buy a house for $900,000, even a seller who isn't as concerned as a bank about your annual income will more than likely stop the conversation and ask you to leave. You may need to look at lower priced homes or you may consider times like that a test of your ability to stay in the game.

You will be able to stay in the game by anticipating both positive and negative seller responses, quickly having attractive alternative suggestions ready to offer the seller, almost no matter the challenge.

Some banks indicate that a home's sale price should not exceed 2.5 times your annual salary. In other words, if your annual salary is $80,000 then you would need to avoid looking at houses that cost more than $210,000.

It may be clear that guideline is far too conservative to result in any meaningful number of home sales. So again, you will benefit most by avoiding banks and talking to sellers about lending directly to you.

Importance of Debt to Income Ratio (DTI)

Most bank and institutional lenders use the Debt to Income ratio to determine whether a home loan applicant would be able to continue to afford payments on a specific property for the foreseeable future.

Learning how to calculate your DTI helps you before and during your negotiation with the seller whether or not a bank is also involved. It will be important for you to know how to measure your own DTI.

DTI is not an indicator of your willingness to make your monthly loan payment. The DTI was created solely as a tool to predict your projected home loan payment's financial burden.

When considering a home loan application, lenders look at your front-end ratio and your back end ratio. The two ratios are factors in your DTI. Your front-end ratio measures how much of your gross monthly income would go toward a home loan payment. Many banks say that a home loan payment should not exceed 28 percent of your gross monthly income. Many buyers find that trying to meet the bank's guideline of 28 percent or less is too restrictive. For instance, if you make $42,000 a year, your monthly house payment needs to be less than $1,000.

$42,000 x .28 = $980

If you know what your home loan payments are going to be, you can also determine your loan's front-end ratio by taking your projected monthly housing expense and dividing it by your monthly income.

For example, if you expect your PITI monthly loan payments to be $1,100 and your gross monthly income is $3,500, you would divide $1,100 by $3,500 to arrive at a front end ratio of 31%.

$1,100 / $3,500 = 31%

This is a lending term that describes the hopeful borrower's monthly debt compared to his or her monthly gross income.

Most bank and institutional home loan guidelines enforce a maximum DTI ratio that is at or above 43 percent. When a bank is not involved, the DTI ratio is far less of a barrier to your eventual home purchase. In a moment you will see how easy it is to calculate the DTI.

With negotiation of contract terms, such as a seller who agrees only to minor repairs, a loan with a DTI above 43 would probably still be acceptable. Since the seller will be your lender, DTI can be much more subjective than it would be with a bank. You will see how much this can work for you in Step 6.

Calculating Income

Traditional lenders calculate income differently than you might expect. For example, there is more than just the "take home" pay to consider. Lenders perform special math depending on the type of bonus income the applicant receives. Traditional lenders also give credit for certain itemized tax deductions and often apply proprietary guidelines to part-time work.

There are many more bank calculations that could make you dizzy. You will want to talk instead to sellers willing to lend. Sellers are almost always far less analytical. Here are more bank algorithms that often stop bank loans from happening:

The easiest income calculations apply to W-2 employees who receive no bonus and make no itemized deductions. Because the W-2 can be relatively simple, here is a look at how that income type is calculated.

If you are a W2 employee and are paid twice monthly, your lender will look at your last two pay stubs, add your gross income and use this sum as your monthly household income.

If you receive bonus income, your lender will average your annual bonus, use it as a monthly figure and add that to the income column or entry box on your loan application.

For self-employed borrowers and applicants who own more than 25% of a business, calculating income is more involved.

To calculate income if you are self-employed, lenders will typically add the adjusted gross income as shown on your two most recent years' federal tax returns, then add certain claimed depreciation to that bottom line figure. Next, the sum will be divided by 24 months to find your monthly household income.

Income that is not shown on tax returns or not yet claimed cannot be used for loan qualification purposes.

In addition, all home loan applicants are eligible to use certain regular, ongoing disbursements for purposes of padding their income. For example, pension disbursements and annuities may be claimed so long as they will continue for at least another 36 months. Social security and disability payments from the federal government can also be used.

Non-taxable income may be used at 125% of its monthly value.

In the next section, we will look at how the debt portion of DTI is calculated, the fact that there are two kinds of debt, and how debt will impact the DTI and the loan decision making process.

Calculating Debt

Not all debt on a credit report must be used, and some debt that is not listed on a credit report should be used.

Recurring debts include such payments as your credit card and vehicle payments. The sum of these monthly debts is known as your back end ratio.

To calculate your monthly recurring debts, add the following figures that apply to your situation:

- Credit card payments
- Vehicle payments
- Personal loan payments
- Student loan payments
- Child support and/or alimony payments
- Other monthly payments that may not appear on your credit report

The sum of your payment figures above is known as your monthly recurring debt.

Several exceptions to the list above may apply. For example, if you have a car loan or other payment with 10 or fewer payments remaining, those payments do not have to be included in your calculation. Student loan payments that have been deferred for at least the next 12 months can also be ignored.

For purposes of the Debt to Income calculation, your home loan payment will include your property tax bill paid on a monthly basis, your homeowners insurance, also calculated as a monthly expense, and monthly association dues, if applicable.

Your back end debt is then added to your front end debt. The sum will represent your total monthly debt.

If you still have questions about "front end" versus "bank end" debt, see the definitions in Appendix B.

70

Calculating Your DTI

After you've determined your monthly income and your monthly debt, finding your Debt to Income ratio is a matter of basic math. Divide your monthly debt by your monthly income.

Here are a few sample ratios using the DTI formula based on 3 different types of income:

DTI of 25%

- Monthly Social Security (at 125%) = $6,000 *

- Monthly recurring (front end) debts = $500

- Monthly housing (or back end debts) = $1,000

- Total monthly debts = $1,500

- DTI formula = $1,500 divided by $6,000

DTI of 35%

- Monthly W-2 income : $7,500

- Monthly recurring (front end) debts: $900

- Monthly housing (or back end debts): $1,700

- Total monthly debts: $2,600

- DTI formula = $2,600 divided by $7,500

71

DTI of 45%

- Monthly self-employment income : $8,800

- Monthly recurring debts : $1,500

- Monthly housing payment : $2,500

- Total monthly debts: $4,000

- DTI formula = $4,000 divided by $8,800

* Remember that non-taxable income can be calculated at 125% of its monthly value.

Most bank and institutional lenders require buyers to have a DTI of 43% or less, but loan approvals are still possible with a higher DTI. In general, applicants with an elevated DTI must show strength on some other aspects of their application.

This can include making a large down payment; showing an exceptionally-high credit score; or having large amounts of reserves in the bank accounts and investments.

Note that once a loan is approved and funded, lenders no longer track the DTI because it's used strictly for loan approval.

Without bank financing, DTI should not be a problem. Follow the advice in Step 6. If the subject of DTI does come up, you will know how to handle it to your greatest advantage.

Before and during your home search, you will find yourself in situations that require you to calculate your DTI ratio, among other important calculations. Here are three sample monthly payment scenarios for one specific house:

Scenario # 1

If you are prepared to offer at least 10% as a down payment, have a monthly income of $3,500 and agree to a 5.5% interest rate, the most you should pay for a house would be $240,000. Your monthly payment would be approximately $1,226.

Scenario # 2

What if you offer the seller a down payment of 20% instead? That means you would give the seller $48,000 for the same $240,000 house so that you would ultimately need to finance only $192,000 instead of $214,000 as above. With 20% down, your monthly payment would be about $1,090.

Scenario # 3

With 30% down, your loan amount would be $168,000. Your monthly payment would be $954.

Now that you have the three scenarios and you know more about DTI, what would the ratios be in each of the next three examples where the total monthly recurring debt was $500 in each case?

DTI Scenario # 1

Monthly Housing Costs = $1,226

Monthly Recurring Debt = $500

Total Monthly Debt = $1,726

Total Monthly Income = $3,500.

What is the DTI ratio for scenario # 1?

DTI Scenario # 2

Monthly Housing Costs = $1,090

Monthly Recurring Debt = $500

Total Monthly Debt = $1,590

Total Monthly Income = $3,500.

What is the DTI ratio for scenario # 2?

DTI Scenario # 3

Monthly Housing Costs = $954

Monthly Recurring Debt = $500

DTI Scenario # 3 (continued)

Total Monthly Debt = $1,454

Total Monthly Income = $3,500.

What is the DTI ratio for scenario # 3?

(Find the correct DTI answers for each scenario near the beginning of Step 3)

Step 2 – The Bottom Line

Now that you have collected, organized and begun analyzing your paperwork, you are getting a much better idea of what size and type of house you have a chance of owning. Once you've completed your initial analysis here in Step 2, you will be in position to put a more convincing presentation together. That's what the next Step 3 is all about.

You will want to become familiar with the material in all 7 steps before you start your search. It may be tempting to begin searching for houses right now, but stop yourself. You are not ready to move on to the search in Step 4 yet. You are not a traditional buyer, so your preparation has to carefully follow all of these steps in order.

Step 3 - Prepare to Present

BE READY TO PRESENT YOUR FINANCIALS

"You can have brilliant ideas, but if you can't get them across, your ideas won't get you anywhere."

-   Lido "Lee" Iacocca

Based on the completion of your document organization in Step 1 and your "interview" with the bank, as well as the improved knowledge of your financial position as buyer from Step 2, you have arrived here at Step 3. Remember that no step should be skipped or done out of order.

Whether you will be presenting your financials to one or more sellers, or anyone else, you will need to be well prepared. Mark Twain once said, "It took three hours to prepare my best impromptu speech."

You need to take time before your first visit to make the best first impression possible in order to convince the seller that you are the right buyer. That won't happen if you rush to talk to sellers before completing Steps 1 and 2. You also need to finish this Step 3.

You may have discovered or already knew that your credit score is less than 550 or your DTI is greater than 48%. You may also know that your down payment is less than 3.5% of the asking price of a specific house you have in mind. Don't let these facts prevent you from continuing with these steps.

These are only factors that would almost certainly guarantee a loan rejection from a bank. That can be depressing, but don't let that discourage you from searching for, and then negotiating directly with sellers. Just remember, sellers willing to lend are almost always more forgiving than banks or institutional lenders. Those sellers will provide you a golden opportunity.

In the steps ahead you will discover various ways of overcoming seller objections based on those traditional roadblocks to acceptance. You are on the right path when you are dealing directly with sellers as your lender and using this book to work with them most effectively.

Speaking of DTI, here are the correct ratio answers to the three sample DTI scenarios at the end of Step 2.

DTI Scenario # 1	DTI Scenario # 2	DTI Scenario # 3
$1,726 / $3,500	$1,590 / $3,500	$1,454 / $3,500
DTI = 49	DTI = 45	DTI = 42

Do you remember which DTI would be most desirable and why? Do you know why your DTI is so important to both of you, even if the seller never asks?

77

Maintain your focus on those sellers that you will find using Step 4. Then, depending on your ability to learn and master Steps 5 and 6, buying a home this way will be the best deal you will ever make in your life.

If you plan to proceed with this Step and the steps that follow, it means at least one of three things.

- You knew you would not qualify at the bank.

- You were already rejected by the bank.

- You did not agree to the bank's terms.

What Order to Present Which Items

This section is going to be dictated by the order of terms presented in negotiations. Those terms will appear here. No need to peek at Step 6. The order of terms is the first of your three basic presentation elements. The other two elements should feature solid answers based on questions that most sellers will have for their prospective buyers.

Sellers will look at you with two thoughts in mind. "How much of a down payment is this buyer capable of giving me?" The next seller thought is, "Is this buyer capable of paying every month until our Note is paid as agreed?" With those three pillars to serve as support for a foundation on which to structure your presentation, you have enough to create an outline. The completed presentation will need to include written proof to the seller that you are the ideal buyer.

Step 3 - Prepare to Present

To begin this step, imagine you are sitting down with the owner of the first house you found that you liked enough to get serious about. You have a written repair list of items you noticed while walking through. You started with small talk and shortly after that, began talking terms.

You say to the seller, "You are asking $225,000. As much as I like your home, your asking price doesn't reflect the cash it's going to take to repair the items that need attention. I'm ready to offer you $200,000 and not ask you to pay for any repairs.

This is one method of opening up the negotiation. Notice that it begins with a discussion about the home's value. Step 6 will go into much more detail. For now, use this brief introduction to see why it's going to be important to show the seller how and why you can afford the monthly payments on $200,000, which would be about $1,000 a month based on other terms you will bring into the discussion later.

For purposes of this Step 3, you should be prepared to present proof that you can pay as much as $1,000 monthly before you even enter the house for the first time. You won't be offering the proof right away, but you should be ready. You should also be prepared for the seller to either show you the exit door when you offer $200,000 or have the seller counter your offer at, let's say, $210,000.

Since you already know what you can and can't afford, you can either reject the seller's counter offer or eventually agree to the seller's higher amount. Once you both agree to whatever the price will be for the home, you will have the proof already prepared that you can pay whatever the monthly payment on the mutually accepted amount would be.

Step 3 - Prepare to Present

What if the seller insists on getting the full asking price of $225,000? No matter how badly you want the house, this does not mean you should surrender your negotiating position. You will see more about ways in which your position can be optimized in the face of challenges when you reach Step 6.

You may have decided to agree to $225,000 based on the proof that you already have (but have not yet shown the seller) that you can afford to pay $1,149 a month. Again, once you agree to the price, that is the time to show the seller the proof that you can afford the monthly payment.

So what exactly will the proof that you can afford the payments look like? You should bring paper reports to your meeting to help the seller feel that you not only did thorough research, but you also went to the trouble of printing them to hand to the seller. Yes, paper would be more difficult than using a laptop, iPad or cell phone. Of course, you should also bring the helpful electronics with you. But paper is one important unique extra you will provide that brings more comfort and security to the seller so it is clear that you are the right buyer.

Because you won't be able to anticipate every price point that might be discussed, you should arrive at the meeting ready to use an online calculator.

Go to this URL:

www.interest.com/mortgage/calculators/mortgage-calculator/

Input whatever basic terms you both agreed on. That may include such terms as a balloon payment.

If there will be a balloon payment due before the end of a 30 year term:

- Click on "Make Extra Payment."
- Input the date of that final payment.

To get the amount of the final payment:

- Click on the "Amortization Table" tab in the upper right.
- Click on the "Monthly" (circle) near the top.
- Scroll to the month before the date of the last payment.
- Copy the balance in the column on the right.
- Paste it into the column on the left under "Make Extra Payment."
- Then click on "Calculate."

The amortization table should automatically recalculate and the table should now be much shorter. It will also accurately reflect each monthly payment as well as the final balloon payment on the date agreed.

If you don't have a portable device capable of displaying the results, then bring with you preprinted individual spreadsheets for each $10,000 of difference in price. As an example, this home's asking price is $225,000. So you would have four separate sheets with prices between $195,000 and $225,000.

81

Step 3 - Prepare to Present

That would be one spreadsheet each for four possible home prices of $195,000, $205,000, $215,000 and $225,000.

Each of those sheets should display the fully amortized payment schedule along with the date of each payment you will make. The seller will especially like seeing the exact dates of his or her future monthly income on a spreadsheet that came from you. Basically you are telling them, "This is what I will do and you can hold me accountable."

Of course, you won't be able to accurately amortize the payments until you know what loan term and interest rate that you and the seller will agree on. If you don't have a capable portable device, you should preprint your spreadsheets using a 30 year loan term and a 5% rate. If you also discuss the possibility of a balloon payment, you will need a loan calculator like the one that is online and previously recommended.

In case you didn't write down the calculator URL:

www.interest.com/mortgage/calculators/mortgage-calculator/

Be Aware:
www.interest.com calls this online software a "Mortgage Payment Calculator." It should more accurately be identified as a "Home Loan Payment Calculator" (refer to the last pages of the Preface).

The Purchase Agreement Worksheet

In order to better understand what issues you will be facing during the purchase process, this would be a good time to take a look at the Purchase Agreement Worksheet. The Worksheet provides a sneak peek at the Purchase Agreement itself, but the Worksheet is easier to read. You can find it online at this URL:

www.BankFreeHouse.com/Books/Forms

You will make Worksheet entries in Step 6 and use your completed Worksheet as a reference in Step 7.

Step 4 - Search and Identify

NOW YOU ARE READY TO LOOK FOR HOMES

"The way to get going is quit talking and begin doing."

- Walt Disney

Because you have taken the time to organize, review your current finances and figure out approximately how much house you can afford, you are ready to start searching. Before you begin searching, you should add an important and unique parameter to your search.

Finding the right sellers

You will be looking for houses with sellers most likely to "carry paper." These are sellers who can and would become your lender. Some seller motivations will be hidden, so identification could be difficult in some cases. Once you have identified a seller prospect, expect to need more than one meeting before you begin talking about specific Note terms.

In general, skeptics of this process are most likely to criticize this step more than any other. Don't let this stop you (see Appendix

Step 4 - Search and Identify

A). Only those hopeful buyers who are persistent will find and close on a house.

Critics might say that there is no good reason why a seller would surrender ownership of the house while keeping their name on that home's pre-existing loan or loans. This is simply not true. When sellers realize the benefits, they choose to go with creative financing.

In fact, there are at least a half dozen different life changing circumstances in which sellers would make that kind of deal. The circumstances are often related to common life challenges such as divorce, job relocation, loss of a job, foreclosure and retirement, to name the most obvious. Keep reading and you will also see that thousands of investors are looking for buyers. Both prefer monthly payment arrangements.

There are two specific circumstances that can add fuel to any of those flammable life-changing situations. If the seller is late or has missed payments and/or the seller has little or no equity, that seller will be very happy to meet a buyer like you. However, as I have stated before in Section E, a seller does not have to be desperate in order to want to make a deal with you. Although most "Subject To" sellers are experiencing difficulties, the other two seller types are not always motivated by urgency, but more often by profit.

Some critics argue that any buyer who makes such a deal is taking advantage of the seller. In the previous paragraphs it should be clearer why you would actually be the seller's savior in some cases and their cash cow in others. There is a good chance you know someone who sees your purchase as an attempt to take advantage. Please have that critic read this introduction to Step

85

4. Make sure they also read Section E that describes the 3 different types of seller financed lending.

So where exactly do you look for these opportunities? There are 9 places shown here that will help you search and find sellers and their homes. These 9 places may lead you to find more of your own sources.

No. 1 – Meeting with All Home Sellers

Most every area has houses for sale that everyone knows about, either because those houses have signs in the yard or because they are listed on the MLS along with exposure on popular real estate websites.

Here's the problem.

Some folks who hope to buy are not comfortable going to open houses and talking about buying without a bank pre-approval in hand. In fact, without a pre-approval, most would not even visit an open house, let alone start a conversation with a seller (or their agent) about buying the seller's house. But that is exactly what you are going to do.

For the most effective results, meet with sellers after reading all 7 steps in this book. After reading, you should also feel comfortable convincing (and showing) the seller's agent that his or her client will make far more money by selling their house to you (remember to show Figure 5).

No method of identifying a seller who is likely to agree to lend to you is better than a face-to-face meeting, especially if that meeting is at the seller's home. Their home is where they are most comfortable, so it stands to reason they would be more open to hearing your explanation of the many benefits they would get if they sell to you and become your lender. If the seller's (listing) agent is at the home instead, don't hesitate to start the same discussion.

The listing agent is trying to be the seller's hero, so that agent may well be open to your suggestion of some kind of offer, especially if the house has been available for two or more months. The sellers and their agent may have already endured dozens of open houses.

No. 2 – Use Direct Mail

There are no ads (like those recommended in No. 3 below) that are more powerful than a highly targeted and personalized letter followed by a face to face meeting. You will want to identify the names and addresses of the sellers of the houses you would like to own. Asking a Realtor who has some experience with this kind of seller contact would be smart, especially since it would be the seller, and not you, who would be paying for your Realtor's efforts.

Although it would be ideal if the sellers have already expressed an interest in offering financing, you do not need to limit yourself if you feel you are ready to convince sellers who have not thought about lending.

If you are not ready, consider having a Realtor who is familiar with seller financing convince the seller. In general, Realtors often have access to more information about home sellers that can be used to identify which ones would be more likely to lend their equity (see the section about Realtor value in Step 2).

This method should be combined with one or more of the other methods to net a larger number of sellers.

No. 3 – Advertise

Whether you use the local newspaper, a weekly sales publication, go online at Craigslist, post to Facebook or use a combination of those media types, some sellers will respond to your ad that simply says, "I would like to buy your house."

There are sellers that may not call because, based on past experience with ads like that, they believe you are going to make a heavily discounted offer.

You should state in the body of the ad that you will make an offer at or close to market value. That should help get the skeptical sellers to call you.

Before sending the ad that includes the words "at or close to market value" you should add the phrase "in many cases." That will help qualify your position and protect your interest before any calls start coming in.

The next source may be one of the best ways to find a great property with affordable terms.

No. 4 – Real Estate Investment Clubs

These organizations now exist worldwide. Walk into a club meeting as a home buyer and you will instantly be as popular as a spring water vendor finding a lost and thirsty tribe in the Sahara desert. These are investors who often wonder where they can find lease option tenants and buyers for their houses.

Instead of listing each local U.S. club, just visit Creative Real Estate online at www.creonline.com. Their international listings are large and growing.

No. 5 – Visit Specialized Websites

Websites that list only sellers who offer financing seems like it should be number one on this list. In reality, there are still too few listings on these sites.

As seller financing and the IDT become more mainstream, pioneering websites like those shown below will continue to grow and list more houses each month than the previous months.

www.SellFinance.com

www.OwnerWillCarry.com

www.owners.com

Even though these sites have been established for several years and provide a decent source of some seller financed listings, you may find you need to supplement the results using other methods described in this section.

The results of a Google search may also list some websites that specifically state they are a source for identifying currently available seller financed properties. Unfortunately, for some sites, this is just a ploy to get you to click on them.

Once you are on the site you will notice that the offerings are usually something else – mostly foreclosures and short sales. In some cases the deception is deliberate, but it is also because seller financing continues to be misunderstood. Some still consider seller carry-backs as strictly in the category of distressed properties, but that perception is quickly improving.

No. 6 – Visit Popular Real Estate Websites

Zillow, Redfin and Realtor.com are some of the more popular websites that feature listings directly from the local MLS boards. Some of those listings will include a statement about the seller's intention to finance the buyer.

However, many seller financing listings that are taken from the MLS will skip that important statement from the seller.

You don't want to depend entirely on these websites and you would benefit from qualified help.

Have a Realtor use proprietary tools and the MLS as your primary source for more accurate data in general and for identifying seller financed offerings specifically.

No. 7 – The MLS (Multiple Listing Service)

Most MLS listings now have a check box that lets the listing agent indicate the seller's willingness to consider financing the buyer. Since you probably do not have access to the MLS, this would be another good reason to enlist the services of a Realtor. A Realtor is able to offer you more willing sellers than you would find during your own web searches.

Unfortunately, even many Realtors are unfamiliar with seller financing. Be careful to ask the Realtor's level of knowledge during your interview. Refer to the section in Step 2 entitled "Which Realtor Will Provide the Most Value" to learn the questions to ask.

Of course the best reason a buyer has to enlist a Realtor's help is that you get all of the many Realtor's services for free. That's because it's customary that the seller pays the seller's agent's commission and the buyer's agent's commission.

If the seller has a Realtor, you will want to get your own Realtor to represent you. Although it is legal in many states to have one Realtor represent both you and the seller, it is not a good idea unless the seller is not represented and agrees to use the services of your Realtor. This can give you some negotiating advantages, just as having the seller's Realtor represent you can give the seller some advantages.

Make sure your negotiation with the seller indicates in your agreement that the he or she must pay all Realtor commissions, which is normally the arrangement in most real estate transactions. As described in more detail in Step 7, you will want to get important terms like that in writing.

Sometimes the websites that advertise open MLS listings will show sellers willing to carry and sometimes the websites do not. You should first learn the factors motivating a seller to finance in order to find the sellers most likely to carry your paper.

No. 8 – Cancelled and Expired Seller Listings

There are many sellers that aren't desperate in almost every location you can imagine. These are sellers who have recently cancelled their listing or have seen their listing expire. These are sellers well worth contacting who are most easily found using a Realtor. That's because cancelled and expired listings usually disappear from the web but are retained on the MLS.

During your search you are going to encounter knowledgeable sellers, such as investors, as well as those who need to learn (ideally from you) about how to maximize their profit. With advice from this section and from Step 5, you will be helping yourself to a better deal while offering help to the seller.

No. 9 – For Rent or For Sale by Owner (FSBO)

Since so many owners who are selling, or thinking about selling, don't know enough about the benefits of seller financing, you should look in places that may be considered unlikely. These will include, but are not limited to, homes for rent and FSBO (pronounced FIZZ-bo) sellers.

While not every rental property is owned by someone looking to sell, some are. Sometimes those owners have given up on finding a buyer through traditional means, but they could be very receptive if you make an attractive enough offer.

Hopeful buyers can also find FSBO sellers online in a number of places at the following URLs:

www.zillow.com/homes/fsbo/

www.fsbo.com

www.forsalebyowner.com

www.homesbyowner.com

www.realtystore.com/bargain-homes/for-sale-by-owner

93

Step 5 - Establish Your Value

THE SELLER MUST BELIEVE YOU ARE THE PERFECT BUYER

"Your challenge is convincing people you can make this work."

- Sean Parker, Napster Founder and First Facebook President

Okay, you have identified a house you want to own. That means that, under the right circumstances, the seller will want to sell to you as well as lend to you.

The more the seller knows or learns about the many benefits of offering you financing, the more likely he or she will be to not only accept, but to accept on your terms.

The best person for the seller to learn from should be you, the buyer. That will give you the best chance of convincing the seller to accept; again, mostly favoring your terms. Before dispensing your knowledge, however, keep in mind the next piece of advice.

First Impression and Beyond

There is a wise old saying. "They don't care how much you know until they know how much you care." In other words, as important as your knowledge is, establishing rapport with the seller is at least as important.

When you want the seller to lend, you should be more warm and complimentary than you might be in a traditional bank loan situation. In contrast, traditional buyers are sometimes advised to be aloof and occasionally critical throughout the process.

There can be a nasty side effect when sellers can't help but fall in love with prospects who show appreciation for the place they worked hard to make attractive. Sellers will often take advantage of your appreciation if you don't keep that tricky balance and remain the poker player you will also need to be.

When your interest in sellers and their situation is genuine, the benefits you both eventually realize will go well beyond a good first impression. As you ask about them, listen carefully and do little talking. To quote successful sales trainers, "There's a reason you have two ears and one mouth." Later in this step, you will learn about what to listen for and what to say in the section about scripts.

Now it's time to put another puzzle piece in place before going any further in this Step.

Three Levels of Seller Knowledge

You should quickly attempt to determine how much a seller may already know about seller financing. In order to make a deal with the best possible house purchase and loan terms, it will be important that you know as much, and preferably more than the seller.

When you get a sense of how much they know, then, in the next blink of your eyes, put them in one of the three following

95

categories: Novice, Intermediate or Advanced. In some cases, this may not be as easy as it sounds, but you should try as quickly as possible to establish the category. It will be an important basis for the conversation that follows.

One Example of the Novice Level

If you love the house but the seller has made no mention of offering to finance, you could be facing your biggest challenge.

You are probably looking at a seller who knows little about the benefits of seller financing. Convincing the seller, or the seller's agent, will be your job, unless you have someone representing you.

One Example of the Intermediate Level

The seller may already be offering to finance the right buyer. However, be warned. There are cases in which the only reason some sellers make that offer is because they heard that making that statement will bring them more potential buyers. So it's possible that this level of seller may really be a novice, which means you may have to work a bit harder than you expected.

After more discussion you will probably find that the intermediate seller is aware that seller financing could be a benefit - but is not sure how. However, if the seller's intention really was only to attract more buyers, you should be prepared for resistance to further discussion about seller lending.

One Example of the Advanced Level

Some written home sale descriptions will include one or more terms that indicate what would make a buyer an acceptable candidate in the seller's eyes. The seller's description of the terms will often let you know that the seller knows what makes a Note valuable. Do not be intimidated. After further reading, you will probably know at least as much as that seller does – and maybe more.

Now that you have a better idea about how much the seller knows, you will be able to choose which of the following bullet points you need to present to the seller to make a case for seller financing and make a case for you as the buyer.

Benefits of Seller Financing

- Defer capital gains
- Maximize the sales price by offering terms
- Keep equity working for you with higher interest rates
- Receive and deposit the cash down payment
- Collect hassle-free income for years
- Your note is secured by the real property whose value you know
- Get more monthly than you would in rent
- Stop worrying about dealing with tenants
- Don't have to chase after rent payments
- No need to deal with property management

- Never have to deal with HOA (Home Owner Associations)

- No longer responsible for maintenance

- Never have to deal with contractors

- No longer pay property taxes or insurance

- If the buyer stops paying, you keep everything and get the house back

- If you need money, you can sell all or part of your Note for cash, usually more easily than selling the house.

Defer capital gains

Capital gains will likely be increasing with time. For this reason, you should expect to see more people looking to avoid paying the gains, which means government revenues will probably drop.

When a seller in California sells a non-owner occupied investment property, they will incur a 25% capital gains tax liability. For example, someone who receives their asking price and collects $400,000 at the close of the sale on their rental will owe the government $100,000. This leaves the seller with only $300,000 to invest. In other words, that $100,000 is no longer available to the seller.

To avoid this, many people use the IRS 1031 exchange. As complex and restrictive as the 1031 can be, the seller is able to defer capital gains taxes indefinitely using this method, moving from one investment property to another. But what about those

98

who don't want to deal with real estate anymore? Is there another way to defer gains?

Sellers can defer capital gains without a 1031

Seller financing is an alternative sellers can use to defer capital gains. Yes, sellers will pay capital gains on the down payment they receive and then they will owe gains tax on the amount of the principal they receive each subsequent year.

However, if they amortize your note over 30 years, they are initially receiving mostly interest payments (which are taxed at the regular rate). There is only a small amount of principal reduction, which means their capital gains liability is minimal for many years.

Another seller carry-back strategy that allows sellers to defer capital gains is the Title Holding (Land) Trust, which has the added benefit of eliminating exposure to the frustration, time and expense of foreclosure. How? If a buyer stops paying on a Land Trust, the buyer's right to the property, known as the beneficial interest, can be terminated quickly and without any legal action. This makes a Land Trust dangerous for buyers.

The Land Trust was mentioned in Section D as one of the 8 other ways to buy a house with no bank loan. Remember that the buyer does not get legal title until the entire Note is paid, which is another serious drawback of a Land Trust and a serious drawback for many of the other non-bank methods.

Next are valuable dialogs you can use with sellers.

Step 5 - Establish Your Value

Sample Scripts

Think of these scripts as brief, entertaining and informative monologues. They are good ways to start the conversation that can result in an ideal house purchase that clearly benefits you and the seller.

Once you explain why and where you are coming from to the person you need to influence, then the only thing left to do is follow the rest of the steps in this book.

Keep in mind that these scripts are short and only meant as an introduction. You must be prepared to immediately elaborate on the script by becoming familiar with this entire book. By doing so, you will accomplish two goals.

First, the scripts will help you thoroughly convince the seller that a carry back is the perfect solution.
Second, you will be able to begin using Step 6 to negotiate specific items and make sure you and the seller go all the way to the closing table.

The scripts will be presented in the following order:

You are the buyer...

1 ... talking to the seller (if seller is not represented)

2 ... talking to the seller's (listing) agent

3 ... talking to your prospective agent

Here are the corresponding scripts:

1. When the seller is not represented:

(Script works in a seller's market; you love the house or both)

"I want to make you an offer to buy your home. Unlike other interested possible buyers who want to negotiate a lower price, I want to offer you your full asking price.

Here is one likely reason why other interested buyers would need to negotiate your price.

Bankers often tell buyers they will not easily afford a home loan. That's because many banks charge high rates and fees.

So by the time those buyers have paid the bank's rates and fees, there isn't enough left over to offer you what you want.

But if we avoid dealing with the bank and I ask you to loan the equity in your house, we will both benefit in five ways.

First, I will be able to offer you your asking price.

Two, you will have years of steady monthly principal and interest income.

Three, you won't have the effort or expense of maintaining the house or paying taxes.

Four, at the closing table, we will share fewer and less costly closing fees.

Five, we will experience a much faster closing process.

These are major benefits that give you what you need and also make my decision to buy your house easier."

2. Talking to the seller's agent:

(Script works in a seller's market; you love the house or both)

I want to make an offer to buy your client's house. Unlike other interested possible buyers who want to negotiate a lower price, I would like to offer the seller's full asking price.

You know very well that bankers often tell hopeful buyers they can't easily afford a bank loan. That's because most of those banks charge high rates and fees. That could be why banker rhymes with anchor.

So by the time those buyers have paid the bank's rates and fees, there isn't enough left over to offer your client what he or she wants. If we avoid dealing with the bank and we ask your seller to loan to me instead, I will be able to offer the asking price.

Your client will have years of steady monthly income without the effort and expense that goes with maintenance, property taxes and insurance.

We will share fewer and less expensive closing fees and experience a much faster close.

3. Talking to your prospective agent:

Although some agents may be familiar with the concept, they often don't know enough about the benefits or how to implement the concept properly.

If you, the buyer, are having trouble convincing your own prospective agent that you could benefit from seller financing, then you should seriously consider finding a different agent. If you prefer to stay with this agent, it will be your job to help the agent understand this kind of transaction so everyone involved in your purchase will benefit.

Read this book cover to cover. If that is not sufficient, recommend that the agent get this book and advise him or her to also read it thoroughly.

Here are some questions you would ask your prospective agent:

- If I asked you to find my ideal house that also has a seller who is willing to become my lender, where would you look?

- What tools would you use to find that house?

- Why would you recommend or reject the idea of buying from a seller willing to lend?

- If I was the one who found such a house, what would you say to the seller to convince him or her that I am the perfect buyer?

103

How to Respond to Seller Hesitation

Be prepared. The would-be seller will probably finish the next sentence with at least one of the following excuses for not selling, or offering to sell, then deciding not to sell:

"I would sell my property but I can't because....

1. ...you can't offer me all cash at the close.

2. I would have to pay large capital gains taxes.

3. I don't want to do a 1031. It's too complicated and time consuming, so I am forced to keep it and try to rent it.

4. I am tired of repairs and having to deal with tenants, but it seems there is no alternative.

5. I would prefer to hold on to the property and be able to leave it to my children.

This is how you should respond to each of those five most common seller's excuses:

1. You would be losing a huge chunk of profit by accepting all cash at the close. Show the seller a print of Figure 5 and be prepared to talk about it.

2. There are few better ways to avoid a large capital gains obligation than to offer me financing. You would only owe the IRS tax on the sum of my monthly payments to you for each individual year after we close.

3. Yes, the IRS 1031 expects you to buy another property so that you can avoid capital gains taxes on the sale of your existing property, and they don't make the process easy. If you knew of a smarter alternative and a safe investment with a higher yield that would allow you to relax and enjoy life, wouldn't you take it? Of course you would, and offering me a home loan is your perfect solution! I am better than a tenant because I will do the repairs and pay the property taxes.

4. When it comes to a point where you don't want to continue taking care of seemingly endless property repairs, lending to me is the better way.

5. Why have your children inherit a property that needs time, attention and property taxes? You can see how much more you would make (and leave to your children) by lending directly to me than to keep the house or sell the house and get all cash at the close. (Show the seller a print of Figure 5)

Be Able to Explain Seller Financing Benefits

You will be more certain that you have the seller convinced that lending is a good idea by using this script. Get familiar with the following script through practice with someone else or in front of a mirror.

YOU: "Once the loan terms are agreed to by both of us, you become known as the beneficiary. That's because you "benefit" from the profit you keep from my monthly payments. It also gives you the ability to foreclose if my payments should stop."

"My monthly payments are not going to stop until the house is refinanced or paid off. That's because I would have thrown away my down payment and all my payments after that. I know I would still need a place to live and, as you can tell, my first choice is to live here. Those are at least 4 important reasons I won't miss any payments."

"Another reason you don't have to be concerned about my payments? We should use an impartial and experienced professional third party to take care of the loan servicing. Many servicers are easily affordable, so agreeing to use one will be an excellent investment for both of us."

"The third party servicer will create and send a complete invoice for each payment to you, me and the credit bureaus every month. I don't want to lose my investment, nor do I want any negatives on my credit reports. So I will work hard to avoid late payments and I will most certainly do my part to avoid giving you any reason to foreclose."

Many home sellers think they need an all cash buyer, but do they? In order to truly maximize their profit, what many sellers really need is steady cash flow (see Figure 5 – "How much more the seller will make").

If a seller received the full asking price, he or she would probably spend some and invest the balance. In most cases, the invested portion would need to be able to provide at least a 6% return on their money. A note secured by their house can provide a solid rate of return and a steady income for years.

Even when money is cheap, some borrowers who might otherwise be excellent buyers still can't qualify by institutional standards. The best candidates for seller financing are most often homes being sold by elderly people who have paid off their home loan, have another place to move to, and could use more monthly retirement income.

There's nothing easier than depositing a note payment. Collecting rent may or may not be effortless, but you still have to deal with tenants, maintain the property and pay property taxes and insurance. If you are receiving payments on a note, all you do is cash the check. With direct deposit, you don't even have to bother making a deposit.

Show This to the Seller

As you can see in Figure 5, the seller who becomes the lender makes much more on the sale of the house than he or she would if the asking price, or the entire negotiated purchase price, was delivered in full at the closing table.

You should print the graphic in Figure 5 and bring it with you to your meeting with the seller. You can find the graphic on the next page and at the following URL:

www.BankFreeHouse.com/Books/Forms

Seller's Traditional Sale VS No Bank Sale

The following comparison is based on a home sale price of $200,000

Traditional Sale
WITH Bank or other Institutional Lender

Minus Expenses of Sale:

AGENT COMMISSIONS	$ 12,000
TITLE INSURANCE	$ 1,100
HALF ESCROW CHARGES	$ 600
COMPLETE APPRAISAL	$ 550
COUNTY TRANSFER FEES	$ 220
MISCELLANEOUS	$ 140

SELLER GROSS:	$185,390

MINUS EXISTING LOAN:	—	$ 60,000

Traditional Sale * SELLER NET:	$125,390

* Remember that seller collects once only!

No New Bank Loan Sale
WITHOUT Bank or other Institutional Lender

Minus Expenses:

ANNUAL LOAN PAYMENTS:	$ 12,160.46
SALE EXPENSES WITHOUT AGENT	$ 2,610.00

Plus Seller's Income:

BUYER'S DOWN:	$ 20,000.00
SELLER'S EQUITY	$140,000.00
ANNUAL INCOME	$ 18,000.00

At Close SELLER NET	$157,390.00
Year 1 SELLER NET	$163,229.54
Year 3 SELLER NET	$174,908.65
Year 5 SELLER NET	$186,587.73
Year 7 SELLER NET	$198,266.81
Year 10 SELLER NET	$215,785.43

Traditional Sale
Total Proceeds to Seller

$ 125,390.00

Based on an interest rate of 4.5%

No New Bank Loan Sale
Total Proceeds to Seller

$ 215,785.43

Figure 5 - How much more the seller will make by lending to you

Step 5 - Establish Your Value

Why should a seller trust you to make the payments? How can you trust that the seller will make all payments to the existing lender on a timely basis?

Solution: Both you and the seller agree to monthly servicing. Here is what you should expect:

Benefits of Professional Loan Servicing

- Monitors Buyer and Seller Payments
- Delivers Monthly Statements
- Notifies All Credit Bureaus
- Enforces Late Fees per the Note
- Prepares Year End Statements
- Internet Access for 24/7 Account View
- Allows Online Pay or Pay By Phone
- Payment Processing (ACH, Check, etc)
- Escrow (Impound) Management
- Handles Tax Reporting

For more about loan servicing, see Steps 6 and 7.

Need More to Convince the Seller?

You and the seller will want to read this article by investor Seth Williams. He is certainly not alone as a seller when he admits that his fear of the unknown almost caused him to miss out on the best method of buying and selling homes.

Why Seller Financing Makes Sense

by Seth Williams

The idea of seller financing used to scare me to death. The idea of "becoming the bank" didn't sound appealing to me AT ALL.

In my mind, I just wanted to be cashed out *as soon as possible* so I could be done and move on with my life. However, once I realized the **truckload** of extra money I could be making as a result of financing my properties; I decided to try my hand at it.

After selling one property, and then another, and then another – I started noticing how nice it was to have checks delivered to my mailbox every month *whether or not I continued to put forth any additional effort.*

Eventually I found that it was adding a lot of stability and predictability to my business operation and life...**and I loved it**.

Before long, I started putting it to use *whenever I possibly could*, and it quickly became my **preferred method of selling real estate**. To be honest, I'm kind of surprised that everybody isn't doing this as a *standard business practice*. The fact is, when you finance the sale of a property, you are creating **a true money machine**.

Offering seller financing will **open the doors of opportunity** and will allow you to work with MANY more potential buyers. The truth is, a lot of buyers won't even consider buying your property simply because they don't have access to the funds they need in order to purchase it. When you offer seller financing, you're solving this problem right out of the gate because *you're giving them the financial leverage they need.*

The more flexible you can be and the more options you can offer your potential buyers, *the faster you will get your property sold* – plain and simple. On the other hand, if you're only willing to get cashed out in one lump sum (and this is how most sellers operate), you could find yourself sitting on your property for **a lot longer than you need to**.

One of the huge advantages of financing your property is that you can almost always ask for a higher price on the property and *many people will pay it.* In my business, I can even charge a higher-than-market interest rate and most buyers don't care!

I'm able to get away with this because I understand how to **make the monthly payment affordable**.

When I advertise my properties with seller financing, *I don't even talk about what the specific terms of the loan will be* (interest rate, payment period, etc.). Of course, this information will be included in my closing documents (I'm not hiding anything from anybody), but when it comes to marketing a property – I've learned that people tend to get confused by all the intricate details of the transaction (and a confused mind says "No"). In the end, all they really want to know is **what it's going to cost them each month**.

With this in mind, I just advertise two things:

1. The total purchase price
2. The monthly payment

That's all.

When people see a monthly payment, they will know whether it fits into their budget – and at the end of the day, *this is all that matters to most people.*

The nice thing about this is, if your goal is simply to make the monthly payment affordable, there is *almost always* a way to make the payments work within a person's budget. Remember, **you are the bank**.

You can stretch out the term of the amortization (aka – the amount of time, or number of months it will take for them to pay you back). You can also adjust the numbers by giving them a lower interest rate. You could require a larger down payment upfront (which will reduce the amount of the loan and thereby, reduce the monthly payment), or you could just lower the price of the property altogether.

Whatever it takes for you to sell your property *and make money*, **do it!** One of my goals with this strategy is to build up SEVERAL streams of income, and this only happens by selling SEVERAL properties with seller financing, in a way that will earn me a profit.

112

When you're the lender, you can generally do whatever you want to (within the law, of course) to *maximize your income* over the long-term.

At the time of this writing, mortgage rates are *as low as they've ever been*...but guess what – even with how low mortgage rates are right now, I am currently able to charge **9.99% interest** on my seller financed properties and *people are happy to pay it!* Why? If I don't finance the property for them, *they can't do the deal*, **period**.

Remember, for a lot of buyers, the interest rate is irrelevant IF they can afford the monthly payment. It's all about making the property affordable for the borrower at a down payment and monthly payment they can live with.

As you start talking with prospective buyers, you'll find that **different things matter to different people**. Some buyers will want a low price, some buyers will want a low payment and some buyers might even want 0% interest. Whatever their sticking point is, *do whatever you can to work with them!* The ultimate goal is for you to make a monthly profit on each sale, so if you can meet their needs AND accomplish your objective, make it happen! Generally speaking, a*s long as your buyer is getting a great value for their money, they'll be happy to do business with you.*

There are a lot of people who are **huge fans** of seller financed property – so when you decide to sell, don't underestimate the power of offering this as an option in your property listing.

The funny thing is, whenever I offer seller financing in my property listings, *almost everybody* chooses to take the financing and NOT pay all cash (even when there is a financial incentive for paying cash). *Even when people have the cash available,* many of them would still rather pay for the property over the long-term and not tie up their funds by paying for everything upfront. It may sound strange, but if you're the type of person who doesn't like debt, then you would probably be surprised at how common this is.

Monthly servicing fees are another way to tack on some extra monthly income from seller financed properties. I always charge a monthly servicing fee of $15 – $25 (this is *on top* of the borrower's monthly principal & interest payments to me).

Why?

With every existing loan, someone must be in charge of:

- Collecting the monthly payment
- Updating the loan balance
- Sending a statement back to the borrower
- Dealing with delinquent accounts

On my first few seller financed deals, I tried to get my feet wet by servicing my own loans in-house.

I had a banking background and I understood how to do it, so the job was something I could do, but personally – I learned that I just didn't enjoy spending my time doing busy work.

Servicing a loan isn't terribly difficult, but it does need to be done right and it takes a lot of left-brain thinking to do the job well. As a result, I eventually decided to outsource my entire loan portfolio to a loan servicing company and let me tell you... they do *a great job*. It has freed up my time immensely and if I could do everything all over again, I probably would have started sending this work to them from day one.

Coincidentally, my loan servicing company charges a monthly fee between $15 and $25 for this service, so rather than me taking the hit for this cost myself, I just pass it along to the borrower. Remember, if it works within their budget (if their monthly payment is still affordable), do it! Just be sure to disclose this in your documentation when you close the loan.

Even if you decide to service the loan yourself, you should *still* be charging this kind of servicing fee to pay yourself for the trouble! As long as you have outstanding loans owed to you, **the job will always be there**, so make sure you are compensating whoever is handling this extra work – **especially if it's you!**

Whenever you close a loan, you'll need to use the right documentation. Whether you decide to close your deal in-house (preparing all of the documents yourself) or use escrow, a title company, real estate agent or attorney, *somebody* has to put the paperwork together.

Regarding the loan servicing issue, *the paperwork isn't going to take care of itself*, so you need to factor this cost into the deal upfront and pay the appropriate person for doing this extra work on a monthly basis.

All of these costs are **very typical** in any type of loan arrangement. I guarantee you a bank would be charging these kinds of fees for a conventional loan.

Step 5 - Establish Your Value

When you're acting as the lender, you can be as flexible as you want to be.

Once the deal is closed, **your borrower owns this property**. As long as they keep making their payments to you, *the property legally belongs to them*.

For instance, in the same way that I wouldn't expect my banker to come and fix my toilet after I buy a house – the borrower shouldn't expect YOU to come out and take care of their property either.

Of course, a seller financed property is a stream of income that won't last forever (because the borrower will eventually pay you off), but believe me – **it's great while it lasts** (and it will usually last for a long time). When I finance the sale of my properties, *I don't have to lose a wink of sleep at night* because once the deal is done; all the maintenance and upkeep issues are in the borrower's lap, not mine.

As soon as you've built up enough cash reserves to run your business efficiently, I suggest that you start financing your properties as soon as possible. I know some real estate investors who make **over six figures per month** *just from the ongoing payments from seller financed properties*. That's right, PER MONTH.

The beautiful thing about the properties I finance is that in most cases, I only paid 10% to 20% of the property's market value when I bought it in the first place. Think about it. If you buy a property for $5,000 and sell it with seller financing for $50,000 – you can make your **entire initial investment** back with just the down payment! Once the loan is in place, every single monthly payment for the next five years will be **pure profit**. How's THAT for your return on investment??

I'll be honest, I personally don't bother with charging prepayment penalties – but I certainly understand the rationale behind lenders that do.

When you enter into a loan agreement with a borrower, part of the reason you're doing this is because you want to create a **dependable** stream of income for a set period of time. If a borrower chooses to pay off their loan prematurely (which some borrowers are sure to do if you are charging 9.99% interest), your stream of income will disappear.

You can't *disallow* this from happening, but one way to *discourage* these kinds of early payoffs is to charge a prepayment penalty. It will also serve to compensate you for your unexpected loss of income.

If you want to add this extra security to your seller financed deals, you should have this written into the language of your loan agreement. There are many different ways of calculating exactly what your penalty could be, but one way is to charge:

- 5% of the original balance if paid off in the first year,

- 4% of the original balance in the second year,

- 3% of the original balance in the third year,

- 2% of the original balance in the fourth year,

- 1% of the original balance in the fifth year.

Step 5 - Establish Your Value

Obviously, nobody wants to deal with a borrower who defaults on their loan. I'll be the first to tell you that **it's annoying**, and depending on what shape they leave your property in – it could even be costly.

That being said, there are also a number of reasons why this risk is *still* very *worthwhile taking*, even when you consider the worst case scenario.

Given how little I typically pay for the properties I purchase, it usually isn't difficult to recoup 100% of my initial investment *just by collecting a 10% – 20% down payment*. Even if you only collected a 5% down payment, you can usually recoup the remainder of your initial investment in the first few months. Essentially, the risk in this area is usually very low.

What I'm getting at here is – if you did your groundwork right when you purchased the property (i.e. – buying for the right price and the right terms), **you're not going to end up in the hole** – not by a long shot.

Now on the other hand, if you borrowed $100,000 to buy the property, and the property was only worth $125,000 – this would obviously be a different story, but as I indicated earlier in this article, the ideal time to use seller financing is when you own a property **free and clear.** You most likely paid a *very low price* for this property in the first place, so if "losing money" is what you're concerned with, don't be! You will find that extracting your initial investment from properties the way we do is **not difficult**.

Think about it this way – you own a long-term, tangible asset. If you're working this business the right way, you own it *without any debt or monthly payments whatsoever.* If your borrower decides to quit paying you tomorrow, that could be a blessing in disguise. It just means that you can repossess the property (which is probably the only real "hassle" of the process), re-list it, and resell it! **You get to keep all of your delinquent borrower's payments and start the process all over again.** Some of the most profitable deals are the ones you get to repossess and resell.

When I first started selling properties with seller financing, *I didn't do any credit checks whatsoever.* Frankly I didn't care who my borrowers were going to be because I knew that if they ever defaulted on our agreement, I stood to make even more money in the long run.

As you can see, there are a lot of reasons why Seller Financing makes sense. Anything that allows an investor to make **abundantly more** profit AND passive income is worth taking a close look at. While it does involve some extra steps, my personal opinion is that *it's almost always worth the trouble.*

119

Step 6 - Negotiate a Win-Win

WORK ON AGREEING TO EACH OF THE TERMS OF THE NOTE

*"Let us never negotiate out of fear, but let us never
fear to negotiate."* - John Kennedy

You have arrived at Step 6 which has some roots in Step 5 where
you convinced the seller to open up a serious dialog with you.
You took stock of your financial situation in Steps 1 through 3
and then you identified your ideal house by following Step 4. In
this step you will get a bird's eye view of the reasons why the
carry back Note almost always provides more beneficial terms
than a bank Note.

Part of what makes the house ideal is the fact that the seller
expressed a willingness to carry. But the paper the seller is
considering carrying has yet to become your house! Although
the seller is willing, you must carefully negotiate specific terms
of the Note in order to thoroughly satisfy the seller as well as
yourself. Only if you are both satisfied will you be able to
proceed to the close. Obvious? Maybe.

It might surprise you to know that even willing sellers who are
aware of Notes are often unfamiliar with the elements of a truly
successful Note. Believe it or not, you will often need to help the
seller understand what makes a Note better. If you are just as
uncertain, you are about to learn enough to help any seller.

This section of the book will give you the knowledge you will need to ultimately convince even the most skeptical seller that you are the ideal buyer. The tips contained in this step will give you the upper hand during negotiations, in some cases, even if the seller has experience creating Notes.

Here is your golden opportunity to not only impress the seller but to get yourself Note terms that could surpass even your own highest expectations

If the holder ever needs to cash out the entire Note, it should be an available option. Nothing should be more important to the seller than the Note's future cash value. Believe it or not, many existing Note holders don't know how important that is, even if the seller never intends to sell the Note. But the seller's circumstances can and often do change, months or years after your purchase.

Some examples of possible gaps in the seller's knowledge of Notes and what you will learn include the analysis of comparable existing Note terms. You will also discover how to neutralize the benefits inherent to Note sellers - benefits that could come back to bite you months or years after the deed had been recorded.

You will also be prepared to explain the superior tax and income benefits the seller will enjoy. For instance, the most basic benefit yields monthly payments to the seller instead of a lump sum that often triggers an excessive capital gains tax liability. You will show how your monthly payments will not only be regular, but they will provide a higher and safer yield than most any other investment.

Negotiation Techniques

There are at least two negotiation techniques you should know. First, there is the Reluctant Buyer method. Second, you should use Negative Phrasing.

The Reluctant Buyer

You will be amazed at the results you get when you use this technique. Very few home sellers will tell you such things as their lowest acceptable price during the first visit. The seller's hope of getting their highest asking price is a mask that covers their fear of losing you as a potential buyer. The better you are at being a reluctant buyer, the faster and more effectively you peel away the seller's mask.

The basic definition of a reluctant buyer is one who is difficult to please and quick to reject the seller's sales pitches. This does not mean that the reluctant buyer needs to be hostile or ruthless. What it does mean is that you are not as eager as the seller would like you to be. You want the seller to know you are not in a rush to buy, even if you are anxious and would love to own the house as soon as possible.

As a reluctant buyer, you would say, "As much as I like what you did with this house, there are other houses that I am considering putting an offer on." The following statement also works well. "My partner would probably disagree, but I could agree to do that."

What to Avoid

You want to avoid turning any negotiation item into an argument, yet that is exactly what inexperienced negotiators do all the time.

Here are a couple of examples of the wrong things to say. Without thinking, you could declare, "The sellers of the other houses I looked at are asking less."

Never put the seller on the defensive.

The seller might respond, "That house is probably not as nice." Even if neither of those statements is accurate, the seller now has the better position in this negotiation, because any response you have would be awkward and likely to make you look even less appealing than you already do.

You might also say, "The other house I was looking at is larger and there are fewer items needing attention."

Again, you put the seller on the defensive. This could be followed by an argument and maybe even a nasty one. The next technique, Negative Phrasing, will help put you in a better negotiating position.

Negative Phrasing

All negotiations are like a game of chess. You need to put the other side in a position to make a move that will give you the advantage when it's your turn to move. Thoughtful negative phrasing can give you that power of "earned and deserved" anticipation. Soon you will have the seller thinking, saying and offering exactly what you need and want.

There is a clear benefit when you put your statements in the form of questions. Statements are often based on false assumptions that can insult the seller and make you appear presumptuous and less appealing. In contrast, questions show respect for the seller, while the seller's responses can be enlightening for both parties. Here is a sample conversation in which your entire dialog uses negative phrasing.

You: Have you been advertising your house for the last few weeks?

Seller: My house has been listed on Zillow and Redfin for the past few months.

You: How's that been working for you?

Seller: Not so well. I did get one offer.

You: When do you plan to close with that buyer?

Seller: I'm not sure the buyer is serious about closing the sale.

You: What were some of the terms you agreed to in the purchase contract?

Seller: To be honest, we discussed the purchase but never put anything in writing.

You: So you expect that they will be back soon with the written agreement?

Seller: They probably lost interest in the deal. Why don't you and I talk and get it in writing?

To sum up, when you master both techniques, using reluctant buyer in the same sentence with negative phrasing that can be most effective. Using both techniques, you would choose the right moment and say, "May I ask you a few questions to see if I would want to buy your house?"

Now that may sound excessively polite, but part of the mastery of these techniques includes using a more gentle approach. Remember that when you make statements, it may be difficult to avoid coming across as arrogant. Statement can alienate the seller and put an end to your conversation.

Practice these two techniques and you will greatly improve your chances of getting more than you expect.

Now it's time to start talking about the terms.

The Purchase Agreement Worksheet

Having looked at this sheet briefly in Step 3, you will want to begin filling in the information based on the following items to be negotiated.

In case you forgot where the sheet is located:

www.BankFreeHouse.com/Books/Forms

You should print more than one copy. Label the first copy "Ideal Terms" and another copy "Actual Terms." You may decide to add other labels to other copies.

While you read through all of the negotiation points in this Step, you will make entries. You may also want to make some changes, so use a pencil with an eraser.

Okay. Ready, set, begin…

The 5 Most Important Contract Negotiation Points

Included in the critical elements of a Note are the basic five items shown below.

Although these items are typical of any bank financed sale, each item is further explained to include the elements of seller finance. These items are the:

1. **Purchase Price** (the face value of the Note)

2. **Down Payment**

3. **Interest Rate**

4. **Due Date**

5. **Monthly Payment**

Before diving into the details of each category, it will be important to know which type of the three housing markets currently exists. Since a neutral market is very rare, one of the remaining two usually dominates.

Buyer's Market or Seller's Market

Many items you will negotiate are going to be influenced heavily by the type of current housing market. Are there more houses for sale than there are buyers? That is known as a "buyer's market" where buyers have the upper hand in negotiations. Do not miss the great opportunities this market has for you - some will be hidden.

History has shown, however, that the opposite is more often true. The seller's market exists when there are more buyers than there are sellers, which means the sellers generally have the upper hand in negotiations. That kind of market is the primary reason home prices have gone sky high in the past hundred years. No need to be overly concerned though. When you implement the advice in this book, and especially in this step, you will be able to gain the advantage in any market.

1. Negotiating the Purchase Price

The most important and obvious conversation will often be the most heated. You and the seller may agree quickly on the subject of overall house value, but don't count on it. Expect many negotiating items to be a struggle, but they shouldn't be unpleasant ones. You may view negotiations as series of nasty arguments. Don't worry. You will learn to treat them as challenges that are fun and rewarding. Remember, these challenges are not available with a bank loan.

The purchase amount you offer can vary widely, especially if your search includes distressed properties. Even if the seller's asking price seems reasonable, you want to find out how much of a discount you can get, but only if you are in a neutral or a buyer's market.

In a seller's market you will want to make your high offer first, especially if you want the seller to lend to you. Don't worry about a high offer. There will be opportunities to negotiate other terms that can reduce your monthly payment – sometimes well below the monthly payment on a lower asking price.

If you still want to grab that purchase price discount, keep in mind that any bargain to be had must be based on items in one or more of these three categories:

- errors in the comps (homes sold)

- deferred maintenance or damage

- seller's late or missing payments

It may seem obvious that the argument in favor of your discount cannot be based on your inability to afford the house. What's the good news? You can almost always find the chance to negotiate based on that short list of legitimate items above. The most common source of a price reduction would be needed repairs, from minimal to extensive, that would qualify as deferred maintenance, or any damage other than normal wear and tear. Include items that will soon need repair or replacement. Adding imminent repairs or soon-to-be-needed replacement of big ticket items, such as a roof, furnace, air conditioner or hot water heater to your "complaint" list are often overlooked discount opportunities, even by seasoned real estate professionals.

Since many seller financed purchases are based on distressed properties, the same negotiating tactic above would not be the only effective strategy you could apply. Depending on the severity of the seller's situation, you could make an offer well below the appropriate market value. This could be true in every type of market.

Maybe you can get an idea of the seller's situation through conversation and the web. Realtors have useful tools beyond the Internet that often help at uncovering the objective truth about a seller's situation to your greater benefit.

Even if you think you have a solid idea of the current market value of the house, you and the seller should have that proof of value in writing. Be aware that there are different types of written proof and not all are equal in value.
Some sellers know that a formal appraisal is the ideal method of determining current market value.

If your seller ever wanted to sell this Note during its term, the purchase price you both agree to would need to be based on a formal appraisal. That's because it would help the seller get a higher price if he or she needs to sell the Note during its term.

As with many items in seller finance, a formal appraisal is not something you or the seller wants to pay for. It is one of those larger expenses associated with an application for a bank home loan. What would be another reason to avoid a formal appraisal? It is generally more beneficial to the seller.

Many sellers who carry paper don't know the future value of a current formal appraisal.

Sellers generally consider the less formal BPO (Broker Price Opinion – see definitions in Appendix B) to be a satisfactory measure of market value. Some sellers believe the valuations found on websites such as Zillow.com or Homes.com to be good enough.

You would usually do well to agree with any seller who has those opinions, because they will, in most cases, be handing you more cash than you even bargained for during and after the Note's start date.

Gathering a list of recently sold houses in the neighborhood is another method of helping to determine value. Each house on the list is known as a "comp." A comp is the shortened name for a "comparable."

The list itself is usually referred to simply as the "comps." In reality, this method is often an even less dependable indicator of value than a BPO, because one person's definition of an appropriate comp may be very different from another person's definition. This is especially true when those people are not BPO certified or licensed appraisers. That could very well work in your favor – and it should.

Any time there is room for interpretation about the value of any item in your contract, the item is ripe and ready to be negotiated. Create a comps list of your own to be ready when your meetings with the seller get serious. It has been said that data can be made to prove any theory. Your comps could get the seller to agree with what you "proved" the house is worth.

The following statement may not sound logical at first.

Whether or not the house is a distressed sale, the lowest purchase price should not be your only focus. You know that you need to make the seller as comfortable as possible with the idea of lending to you. Therefore, in some cases, you should go ahead and offer the seller their full asking price. There are times when you may even offer more!

Full price can give the seller great comfort, but just the thought of that could cause you to lose sleep. Yes, you may even develop insomnia - unless you realize that you have the ability to manipulate your monthly payment to be the same or sometimes even lower than the monthly payment based on a discounted offer.

As more negotiating terms are revealed below, you will see how those terms can be combined so that each will have an impact on the monthly payments. You and the seller can ultimately agree on an acceptable monthly payment, almost no matter the asking price.

Remember, the seller will be most happy to get a full price offer. You will want the lowest monthly payments possible. The concept of the low payment being as important, or more important, than the asking price is another important reason seller financing became popular.

Before talking more about the monthly payment, you will need to consider other important terms.

2. Negotiating the Down Payment

This critical issue will usually have the second biggest overall impact on your negotiations. There are many ways to use the amount of your down payment to your advantage, whether or not you have at least ten percent of the purchase price.

As with any home purchase negotiation, the higher your down payment, the more favorable negotiating options will be available to you. What is the basic benefit of a larger down payment? The higher the amount you can offer the seller up front, the more of a discount you can negotiate on the purchase price, even if the seller had been firmly against a lower price.

The advantages of a higher down payment are not limited to reductions on the purchase price. In fact, you can use nearly any additional amount of a down payment as a bargaining tool for closing costs and anything from repairs to including the seller's artwork.

Be aware of, and understand the reasons for the seller's most common expectation of a minimum of ten percent as a down payment. Not many sellers could sleep at night if they thought you did not have enough to lose and, at any point, your monthly payments could stop and you could disappear.

Some sellers know that, in case they need to sell during the term of the Note, the Note's future value will be most favorably affected by their buyer's large down payment. Note buyers consider a low LTV (Loan to Value) to be the most attractive Note feature. The smaller the loan balance, the better the Note.

Sellers are generally advised to accept no less than ten percent down from you, but some sources recommend that sellers collect higher amounts. There are a few sellers who might insist on twenty five percent down. Again, don't worry.

From your point of view, no specific amount of a down payment should be an obstacle to successfully negotiating your house purchase.

Just be aware that the less you offer down, the more creative and persuasive you will have to be about how you will compensate the seller in other ways.

You could offer items or services the seller values. You might have to concede other terms, such as repairs you hoped the seller would agree to cover (see also "sweat equity" below). What about closing costs you asked the seller to pay but the seller refused? That would be one instance in which you should remind the seller that a favor is owed to you.

Negotiating the Down Payment
Bank Restrictions

Keep focused on the creative opportunities in front of you and the seller. If you were depending on a bank financed home loan, the typically harsh restrictions on your down payment would be excessive enough to crush the purchase, often before you even begin the written application. Remember that a bank loan would offer you little or no chance for creativity.

If the bank was going to reject you because your down payment is smaller than they require, they might let you borrow from friends or relatives. But the bank would consider that a "gift."

In most cases, the gift would have to be "seasoned" before it could be considered acceptable as a down payment. Seasoning means the money from your relatives or friends would need to have been in your account for at least two months before being used for the down payment.

In contrast, sellers are not going to make such demands, as long as the money is available.

Negotiating the Down Payment
Sweat Equity

Are you at least somewhat handy with tools? Another bargaining issue that is often used to reduce the down payment in seller financing is sweat equity. There is almost always some type of maintenance or repair that the seller's property needs before the sale is final. Not all of this work will require licensed contractors.

Negotiate a reduction in the down payment in exchange for offering to take care of the problem. Of course, your negotiation is not limited to reducing the down payment. Buyers have also negotiated the purchase price, interest rate and any number of other items by offering sweat equity.

3. Negotiating the Interest Rate

Your rate will be one of the most important terms of your agreement. How important? For every quarter percent drop you are able to negotiate in your interest rate, you can afford about $10,000 more in your purchase price.

In the example in Figure A below, your monthly payment will be fixed at about $1,865, whether the purchase price is $360,000 or $400,000. How can that be? Here is an example of how that would work:

NEGOTIATE YOUR INTEREST RATE					
Featuring Principal and Interest Payments					
Rate					
5.25	$2,208	$2,154	$2,096	$2,044	$1,988
5.00	$2,148	$2,094	$2,040	$1,986	$1,932
4.75	$2,086	$2,034	$1,982	$1,930	$1,878
4.50	$2,026	$1,976	$1,926	$1,874	$1,824
4.25	$1,968	$1,919	$1,869	$1,820	$1,771
4.00	$1,910	$1,862	$1,814	$1,766	$1,719
3.75	$1,852	$1,806	$1,760	$1,714	$1,667
HOME PRICE	$400,000	$390,000	$380,000	$370,000	$360,000

Figure A – How much more house you can buy at a lower rate.

Here is another fact that might shock you. Are you sitting down? Good. Buyers have successfully negotiated a ZERO percent interest rate with sellers! Try that with a home loan from a bank! The reasons for negotiating zero percent will become clear shortly.

In the meantime, use the rate comparison examples in Figures B and C to get a better idea about what a zero rate could mean for you over the life of the loan. (No down payment in these cases)

INTEREST RATES

Comparison of sample 15 and 30 year loans
at 5 and 5.5 percent

	15 year	30 year
Interest rate	5 %	5.5 %
Purchase price	$129,057	$129,057
Monthly payment	$1,021	$733
Total interest	$54,646	$134,741
Total P&I payments	$183,703	$263,798

Figure B – How loan rates would affect your payments

In Figure B, at the end of your last year of payments on a 15 year loan for a house worth $129,057, you will have paid almost $55,000 more than that purchase price you agreed to pay the seller. On the house you both agreed was worth $129,057, you will instead have paid a staggering total of $183,703 by the end of the loan term.

136

In Figure B, at the end of your last year of payments on a 30 year loan, for a house worth $129,057, you will have paid an additional $134,741. On the house you both agreed was worth $129,057, you will have instead paid $263,798.

Figure C shows you will have paid no interest at all over the entire 15 or 30 years. You will have paid the seller no more than the purchase price of $129,057.

NO INTEREST

Comparison of sample 15 and 30 year loans
at zero percent

	15 year	30 year
Interest rate	0 %	0 %
Purchase price	$129,057	$129,057
Monthly payment	$717	$358
Total interest	$0	$0
Total P&I payments	$129,057	$129,057

Figure C – How a zero rate affects your payments to the seller

Since zero percent is as low as it gets, the seller is not likely to agree unless you have offered something else of value.

The first negotiable item that most sellers would swap for a low or zero interest rate would be an increase in the purchase price.

The second choice would probably be a down payment that the seller agrees is generous enough.

Other items would include a trade for expensive repairs or renovations. There have been owner financed homes with fire damage. After the fire, the family may have moved into another house soon after the home insurance claim proceeds had been paid. The seller may or may not have intended to do the repairs before offering the damaged house for sale.

Down payment and damage are certainly not the only major bargaining tools that you may have. If your creativity is thoroughly exhausted and you feel you are completely out of tools to offset the higher interest rate, then consider this. If you can afford to make higher payments over a shorter term, you will save a bundle on interest over the length of the loan.

As you will see in the next section, you will also be able to use the loan term (the length of the contract) as another tool to influence the seller's decisions.

4. Negotiating the Loan Term

In the previous section, the examples given in Figures B and C featured a loan term that was limited to either 15 or 30 years. These two time frames are common among home loans from a bank. They are not as common in seller financing and were only offered to highlight the interest rate differences.

Seller financing usually features a term that is more similar to an adjustable rate mortgage, which is best known as an ARM. Those types of loans feature fixed interest rates for periods of 3, 5, 7 and 10 years. With the passage of Dodd-Frank, 5 year loans are the minimum that seller finance is allowed to offer.

The new minimum is good protection for buyers. In the past, the three year seller financed loans that required full payment at the end of that term were found to be unrealistic and damaging to buyers. Buyers were losing not only the house, but all of the money paid during the Purchase Agreement.

Negotiating the Loan Term
The Balloon Payment

Sellers who finance only one property each year are still free to negotiate almost everything else. Although sellers are even allowed to include balloon payments, as they often do, you can agree to the balloon, decline or otherwise negotiate it.

What is a balloon payment? At the end of whatever term (number of years) you and the seller agree to, the entire unpaid balance of the loan will be owed by you. This may not be as negative as it sounds for you. The advantage of a loan with a balloon is the lower monthly payment, since the loan is usually calculated based on a thirty year term and not the actual five, seven or ten year term.

Sometimes, when the term ends, there are buyers who find it difficult to pay the balloon balance. Time can often move more quickly than anticipated.

Most buyers who have agreed to a balloon have reason to hope or expect they will qualify for a bank refinance. If all goes according to plans, you will qualify to refinance, using the bank's proceeds to pay the seller in full. The bank then becomes your new lien holder. But those plans can be too optimistic in the relatively short time frame of five years.

Proceed with caution. See more about the balloon payment later in this step.

In the previous section's Figures B and C, you saw the difference that the change in the length of years made on the size of the monthly payment. The benefit of the longer (30 year) time frame is the lower monthly payment. The longer term in seller finance would be more like 7 or 10 years. Choosing 15 or 30 years may be unusual but they are not out of the question, especially if you reject a balloon.

Term is one of the more powerful items you will be negotiating. If you need lower payments, add as many years as you and the seller agree to.

5. Negotiating the Monthly Payment

Of all the terms in a house purchase, sometimes it seems that an affordable monthly payment is most important to the buyer. Its importance appears to be more intense when the seller finances the buyer's purchase. Is that true for you?

You have seen how all four of the previous items have an effect on the size of your monthly payment. You also saw how each of those items affects the other. So now is a good time to review those items with the focus on the monthly payments.

When your budget is so tight that the monthly payment is the most important factor in your purchase, then you will need to start with a figure and work backwards.

If you truly cannot afford one penny more than $1,100 a month, then the purchase price, the down payment, the interest rate and the due date have to be negotiated separately or in some combination to produce that monthly payment or lower. How can you keep your monthly payment under $1,100?

Negotiating the Monthly Payment
An Example

The seller is asking $100,000 and offering a 6% interest rate for a term of 7 years. You have $5,000 for a down payment but the seller expects $10,000.

If you are unable to increase your down payment, your monthly payment based on these terms will be $1,388. That is unacceptable since you need to keep your monthly payment no higher than $1,100.

You can talk to the seller about accepting a term of 10 years so your payments would drop to $1,055. You might have to offer a solid incentive to get the seller to increase the term. The seller may agree to 10 years, but only if you agree to monthly payments of $1,200 after the seventh year. The seller may also insist those higher payments would not shorten the 10 year term. The seller would keep the additional profit after the seventh year, but your

141

payment for 7 years would be below $1,100. This is one method of reducing your monthly payment.

What if the seller refused to accept a 10 year term and insisted on 7 years? You won't give up because you want that house.

In your struggle to meet the seller's demands, you were somehow able to find another $5,000 for your down payment. Well don't just tell the seller you are now able to increase your down payment from $5,000 to $10,000. Make the seller work for it by matching that larger down payment with your expectation of a $10,000 reduction in the asking price. After all, the seller owes you a favor after insisting on a 7 year term.

If the seller agrees to your purchase price of $90,000, your monthly payment would be $1,169. That payment is still too high, so you would need to work on another aspect to meet your monthly payment goal.

Now you begin looking at reducing the interest rate. You know that with this $80,000 loan at 6% and given the other terms as they are now; your monthly payment would be $1,169. Your budget already told you that monthly amount won't work.

Why would you expect the seller to agree to a lower interest rate? One of the most effective methods would be as follows: You tell the seller that you will drop your request for repairs. Remind the seller that (in most cases) he or she would save thousands of dollars. In exchange you want the interest rate to be 4%. That rate brings your monthly payment down to $1,094.

There are sellers who would accept the reduction, even if they hesitate at first. There are also sellers who will reject your request. Then there are those who would counter. The seller might say, "I will agree to reduce the rate, but only to 5%."

Your monthly payment at 5% would be $1,131 which is not good enough. So you counter at 4.5%. Then your payments would be $1,112, which would be acceptable to you. Prior to the seller's response, this would be a good time to remind the seller that a 4.5% rate means an additional $13,400 in their bank account. So there is a better chance that 4.5% will also be acceptable to the seller.

Other Negotiable Contract Points

Negotiations are certainly not limited to the basic five terms listed above. Take advantage of the creativity that is built into a direct negotiation with the seller using the additional terms suggestions below.

    A. Due on Sale

    B. Balloon Payment

    C. Late Charges

    D. Prepayment Penalty

    E. Closing Costs

    F. Homeowner's Insurance

    G. Contingency Periods

A. Due on Sale

Your seller may want a "Due on Sale" provision in your Note. The smart seller will want to add at least one of two future assurances from you before agreeing to sign your Note. This first assurance would read something like this. "If you sell the house during the term of the Note, the seller (the Note holder) will expect payment in full from you." If the seller doesn't ask for a Due on Sale, or if you reject the request, then your seller/Note holder may ask for the opportunity to evaluate the credit and financial strength of the new borrower, in case you decide to try to sell at any time during the term of your Note.

Your seller may want the future ability to approve or reject your buyer. Like all other Note terms, your obligation is to accept, reject or counter any seller request. You should counter any seller demand to include a due on sale clause. Also, do not give the seller the right to reject your future buyer.

By delivering your verbal objection, or written counter offer to the seller, the balance of negotiating power favors you. What might be your next move?

You should demand an "assumption" clause be included in your Note. This is essentially the opposite of a due on sale clause. The assumption would state that, if you found a qualified buyer, that person would replace you as owner, buyer and borrower.

You may have already rejected the seller's demand to evaluate your choice for a future potential buyer.

Even if your seller doesn't demand the due on sale clause be included, it may not be an issue. After all, you would likely pay the balance to the seller when your sale closes anyway. However, it would benefit the seller to have that in writing.

What should you do if your seller doesn't make either of those demands? That would clearly be in your favor, so don't even bring it up.

B. Balloon Payment

The seller wants a balloon payment due from you at the end of the Note. What is a balloon payment and what does that mean to you? At the end of whatever term (number of years) you and the seller agree to, the entire unpaid balance of the loan will be owed the seller by you. What should your response be?

First of all, you should be aware that sellers are no longer legally allowed to demand a balloon payment if they have seller financed one or more other properties in a twelve month period. If you have already asked the seller whether he or she has financed any other properties within the past year and suspect that the seller is not being entirely honest, there are tools that many Realtors have access to that can help uncover the objective truth about the seller's background.

In any case, you should reject the balloon payment. There is a reason the "balloon" has recently been added to the list of shady home loan practices. No lender should be able to put borrowers in a position where the buyer is facing a wall at the end of the loan term, especially at the end of shorter loan terms.

Negotiating a seven or ten year term would give you a better chance of being able to refinance at the end of the term. As mentioned before, if you agree to a seven year term, tell the seller you would agree, not to a balloon, but to a somewhat higher monthly payment after the seventh year.

The seller would likely agree to your request because of the additional profit. Then, during years 7 to 10, you would have given yourself some breathing room. You could search for the best refinance if you had not already been able to pay the seller off before that.

Your best strategy should include anticipation of a seller demand that you make a balloon payment. By being proactive and checking with Loan Originators before meeting with any sellers, you should be able to get a better idea about what you may need to do to improve your chances of being able to refinance after five, seven or ten years of payments to the seller.

You may be pleasantly surprised at how much more qualified you are than you thought.

C. Late Charges

Most sellers will not miss an opportunity to include a penalty for a late payment. A common seller demand is a late charge of 5% of the payment if it is not made within 10 days of the payment's due date.

Since 5% of a $1,100 payment is $55 and it would be due in just over one week, you would object. The amount is high and the grace period is too short.

As with every negotiable item, your response to the seller's counter offer, if there is one, should be below your acceptable result. So, even though you would accept $45 as a flat late fee charge, you counter with $35 and a grace period of 3 weeks.

If the seller doesn't agree to $35 and 3 weeks, but counters with $45 and 2 weeks, you grouch about it, but you accept.

D. Prepayment Penalty

Since the seller is going to be the Note holder, the seller may be very well aware that much of the Note's profit will be realized over time. If you suddenly have the means to pay the Note in full, then the Note is not as valuable to the seller as it had first appeared.

If, at any time, you are able to make a substantial additional payment that reduces the principal balance by more than 10% in any given year, you might understand why a seller may consider a fair penalty to be half of the lost principal.

Some sellers will demand hefty prepayment penalties to ensure the Note's profitability. Most of those demands will be excessive, so be ready to negotiate or even reject them.

Clearly, no penalty would be best from your point of view. If the seller won't back down, an example of a fair penalty would be 5% of the loan amount or two loan payments. An example of an excessive penalty would be 15% of the loan amount. Another excessive penalty would be one year of loan payments.

In general, penalties should have an expiration date. If your seller is insisting and you just can't eliminate the penalty, make sure you sign the Note only if any prepayment penalties expire no later than 3 years after you and the seller sign the Note.

There are many ways that sellers might structure a prepayment penalty. Watch out for these terms:

- 5% of the original balance if paid off the first year
- 4% of the original balance in the second year
- 3% of the original balance in the third year
- 2% of the original balance in the fourth year
- 1% of the original balance in the fifth year
- No prepayment penalties after year five

As with many of these negotiable items that favor the seller, you should not be the first to mention a prepayment penalty at all. If it isn't already in your unsigned Note, don't bring it up.

E. Closing Costs

Seller financing eliminates many of the closing costs associated with bank home loans. Costs for closing a house sale with a bank loan are usually between 3% and 5% of the purchase price. When negotiated properly, seller financing closing costs should be between one half and no higher than 2%.

Before talking about how to negotiate closing costs, how are they defined? Closing costs are generally shared one-time expenses payable on the day your house purchase becomes final. The amounts you and the seller owe will depend on your previous closing costs agreement with the seller.

Depending on how well you negotiated other terms, sellers can, and sometimes do, agree to pay all closing costs. The seller may surprise you, partly because those costs can be relatively small when no bank is involved.

Although they are smaller, closing costs are no less important than other negotiable items. How important? They appear on page 1 of the latest U.S. loan form called the Loan Estimate, formerly known as the Good Faith Estimate, which was better known as the GFE (see Figure 4).

Keep in mind that closing costs may include the initial payment on recurring costs as well.

What is the definition of recurring costs? They are regularly occurring costs with a specific future time frame and frequency. All recurring costs known at the time of the close are usually scheduled to be paid monthly after the close. All costs should be described in your closing paperwork.

There are several ways to make sure these costs are as low as they can be. First, you should have the seller pay as many of the expenses as possible.

Remind the seller that paying your closing costs is tax deductible. For any of those costs the seller still absolutely refuses to pay, consider increasing the purchase price. The seller will always agree to that, but make sure the purchase price increase is no larger than the specific closing cost the seller is unwilling to pay.

Another way to keep your closing costs low? Schedule the close so it takes place at the end of the month. When the close happens at the beginning of the month, you would owe daily interest from, for example, the 4th until the 30th which, at $7 a day, would be almost $200. If you close on the 29th you would only owe $7 or one day of interest.

Examples of closing costs you should never see in your seller financed transaction are loan origination fees and discount points. Banks expect these to be paid at the close. Sellers never even ask for them.

Examples of recurring costs on a bank loan include mortgage insurance (in many cases). These monthly premiums are also charges you should never see.

Although not all closing cost items will apply (and there may be new additions before the close) here is a basic list of your estimated seller financed closing costs based on a house purchase price of $150,000:

Closing Items and their Estimated Costs	
• Formal Appraisal (often buyer paid before close)	450
• Credit Report	25
• Settlement Agency Fee (usually an escrow firm)	550
• Title Company Search Fee (included in Seller's Policy)	--
• Survey Fee (not always required)	150
• Flood Determination	25
• Courier Fee	15
• Lender's Policy Title Insurance (Seller's Title Insurance)	N/A
• Owner's Policy Title Insurance (Your Title Insurance)	700
• Natural Hazards Disclosure Report	125
• Homeowner's Insurance (included in Impound Deposit)	--
• Buyer's Attorney Fee (Judicial States – Seller Paid)	--
• Lender's Attorney Fee (Judicial States – Seller Paid)	--
• Buyer's Realtor Commission (Seller Paid)	--

• Seller's Realtor Commission (Seller Paid)	--
• * Impound Deposit (Property Taxes and Homeowners Insurance)	250
• Transfer Taxes (dependent on local law)	50
• Recording Fees	50
• Processing Fee (associated with bank loans)	N/A
• Underwriting Fee (associated with bank loans)	N/A
• Loan Discount Points (associated with bank loans)	N/A
• Prepaid Interest (dependent on closing day of month)	--
• Property Tax (see Impound Deposit above)	--
• Wood Destroying Pest Inspection	50
• Homeowner Association Transfer (varies - may not apply)	--

Figure D – What you should expect from closing costs

* If an impound account (a.k.a. escrow account) had been agreed to, it represents a one-time expense. The account itself will be a recurring expense, usually paid monthly.

This total closing costs estimate of $1,265 in the chart above assumes no further negotiation on your part.

The final total will vary, but not by much. Use the amounts in the chart as a basic estimate for expenses. Those costs may be somewhat different from the closing costs in your area.

F. Homeowner's Insurance

Seller financing complicates this otherwise simple choice. To buy or not to buy (a home insurance policy). You will wish it was that easy.

When the seller is not the lender, it usually is that easy. Since there is no bank involved and no bank rules apply when the seller is financing your purchase, it may be tempting to refuse the extra expense.

If you do the right thing and negotiate the purchase of the insurance, here are some of the issues you will be facing.

- Should buyer or seller be the named insured?
- Must the named insured pay the premiums?
- Who will be able to report a claim?
- Who should receive a claim disbursement?
- How will claim proceeds be properly distributed?

You just have to choose from one of two methods that will answer the issues above. These two methods appear in Appendix A. Check out the section of Appendix A labeled Criticism # 5.

G. Contingencies and Deadlines

Since time is often one of the seller's main concerns, you, as the buyer, should make your contingency periods as short as reasonably possible.

What is a contingency period? In the case of real property, a contingency is an item that must be secured or an event that must take place before the home sale transaction can be closed. A contingency period is a previously agreed upon number of days that both buyer and seller are allowed before the contingency is completed to the satisfaction of all parties.

Although it is especially comforting to the seller, shorter contingency periods benefit both of you. The sooner you complete a contingency, the more trustworthy and serious a buyer you appear to the seller. Shorter contingency periods also translate into faster ownership for you.

Traditional sales usually feature at least three types of contingencies - appraisal, loan and inspection. With seller financing, an appraisal contingency is only a possibility. If you were unable to avoid a seller demand for an appraisal, you should demand that the contingency period to be no longer than five days.

Seller finance type sales have fewer contingencies and their deadlines should be shorter than those of traditional sales. If there is a loan contingency in seller finance, it would look very different. For example, the seller might demand 7 days to fully determine your ability to repay before agreeing to accept monthly payments from you. You can counter by allowing for 4 days, but if you followed Steps 1 through 5, you can expect no contingency demand.

On the other hand, you may only feel comfortable if the seller allows you at least 14 days to inspect, with the right to cancel at any time up until the deadline.
Missed contingencies could mean penalties like contract cancellation. To inspire confidence, you should offer the seller a per diem if the sale closes late, so the seller gets compensated for each late day. Of course, you do not want to be late and have to pay.

Both parties should agree that if you can't close on a certain date, the seller will automatically extend the contract for, as one example, up to 15 more days. If that happens, expect it to cost you anywhere from $20 to $75 per day until it's closed.

The Importance of Note Terms

As the buyer, you need to be aware of what makes your home loan (the "Note") valuable to the seller. Even if the seller is only somewhat aware, this knowledge will help you understand at

155

least some of the reasons the negotiations will go in a certain direction. With this knowledge, you will improve your ability to influence the negotiation of the Note.

The value of the Note benefits largely from the lowest possible Loan to Value (LTV). You should know that sellers are usually advised to require no less than 10% of the purchase price as a down payment. Your higher down payment immediately lowers the LTV and raises the value of the Note.

Since the ideal down payment would be 20% or more, sellers are often told to expect that a Note with less than 20% down will seriously reduce the Note's resale value. They are told there is no substitute for a higher down payment, also known as protective equity.

While it is true that sellers need to be able to protect their interests even if the buyer defaults on the Note, don't hesitate to remind the seller how much you stand to lose as well.

The fact remains that the higher the down payment, the higher the Note's value if the Note ever needs to be sold for cash. Be aware of this so that you expect headwinds when negotiating a lower down payment. Be ready to offer something else of value if your available down payment is low.

The seller is also generally advised that the interest rate on a Note, in most cases, should be no less than the current rate in the market at the time. It should often be a point or two higher. Remember that, even with a higher interest rate, you, as the buyer should still have a lower overall monthly payment. You will also be saving cash at the closing by not having to pay broker or bank points or loan origination fees.

In certain areas, a seller carry back Note is not subject to usury limits. Usury means charging a rate of interest that exceeds the maximum interest rate allowed by law. When it is not illegal, usury can have serious tax consequences. To assure you are getting a reasonable rate prior to the negotiation, ask an accountant for the current IRS imputed home loan rate. The response should justify your position.

The following may surprise you. To minimize the seller's discount in the event the Note needs to be sold, it is important to understand that the due date should be even more important to the seller than the interest rate or the monthly payment. That's because a dollar received today is more valuable than a dollar that will be received in the future - known as Future Value or FV (see Appendix B for a complete definition of Future Value).

In essence, the sooner the Note is due in full, the more the note is worth today. However, the seller can no longer legally offer you less than a five year term. In most cases, you should negotiate a longer term if a lower monthly payment is important to you.

As a buyer you would generally want:

1)   No due-on-sale provision.

2)   If you ever consider reselling during your term, you would want the Note to be assumable.

3)   No balloon payment, unless you are fairly certain you can pay or refinance the balance at the end of the loan term.

4)   No (or minimal) late charges.

5)   No prepayment penalties.

6)   The seller to pay all closing costs.

A compromise might look something like this:

1)   A due-on-sale provision will give the sellers some control in the event the buyers try to sell.

2)   Allow the seller to approve your buyer.

3)   A balloon payment in 7 or 10 years, not 5.

4)   A late charge of five percent of the payment if not paid within fifteen days.

5)   A prepayment penalty only if the buyers make additional payments that reduce the principal balance by more than 10% in any given year.

6)   Seller agrees to pay most closing costs or (worst case) you share closing costs equally.

The Importance of the Letter of Intent

If you still haven't successfully convinced the seller that it's a good idea to be your lender, you should not just give up and walk away. In those cases, you should leave the Letter of Intent as a smart and constant reminder that you offered to buy the seller's house.

Do NOT leave your signed Purchase Agreement (PA) with a seller unless the seller signs it immediately. Leaving it is a mistake that buyers make. Some Realtors have also made this mistake. If the seller signs that Agreement several weeks or months later, you can be legally bound, even if you forgot the Purchase Agreement exists!

If you find yourself wanting to make offers on more than one house, use a maximum of 3 Letters of Intent open simultaneously at any one time. Why? If you change your mind about that house you should remember to immediately notify those sellers holding your Letters of Intent that you need to cancel.

The reason I say "should remember" and not "must remember" is because the Letter of Intent is not binding. That means cancellation is a courtesy, not a requirement. Letting the seller know your position would be appreciated. You may find yourself needing the good faith of each seller you have met. If the currently signed Purchase Agreement does not result in a closed deal for you, one or more of the sellers you spoke with in the recent past who still haven't sold may again be interested in having you buy their house.

The sample Letter of Intent appears in Figure E.

Step 6 - Negotiate a Win-Win

Letter of Intent to Purchase
March 7, 2016

Bernard Woods, Seller
4321 Random Blvd.
Somecity, ST 12340

Michael Jones, Mary Stone, Buyers
123 Anywhere Street
Anytown, ST 12345

Dear Mr. Woods,

The purpose of this letter is to set forth some of the basic terms and conditions of the proposed purchase by us, the undersigned as "Buyers" of real estate owned by you, the "Seller." The terms set forth in this Letter will not become binding until a more detailed "Purchase Agreement" is negotiated and signed by all of us, including the terms below.

DESCRIPTION OF PROPERTY:
The property proposed to be sold is located at 456 Somewhere Avenue, Anytown, ST 12345.

The Real Estate is subject to public highways, covenants, restrictions and zoning, if any.

1. Included are all permanent fixtures and all property that integrally belongs to, or is part of the Real Estate, whether attached or detached, such as light fixtures, and awnings. Our agreement specifically includes the washer and dryer but excludes the living room drapes.

2. PRICE: The proposed purchase price is $150,000 of which $8,000 would be deposited with the escrow agent, upon acceptance of a binding Purchase Agreement. At a 5.25% interest rate, Buyers will pay Seller $784.13 monthly for 7 years. In the absence of a mutual agreement to extend the term of this loan at the end of 7 years, the remaining $123,156 will be due and payable.

3. POSSESSION: Possession would be given on March 14, 2016 or sooner by mutual agreement. Settlement would be made at the closing, immediately prior to possession.

CONFIRMATION OF DELIVERY followed by RECEIPT

_____   _____
Buyer Creating the Letter - Print Name & Sign   Date

_____   _____
Buyer Creating the Letter - Print Name & Sign   Date

_____   _____
Seller Received the Letter - Print Name & Sign   Date

Figure E – The sample Letter of Intent

Buy a House with No Bank Loan   Dean Harris

Step 7 - Get It in Writing

USING THE LEGAL AND APPROPRIATE PAPERWORK

"A verbal contract isn't worth the paper it's printed on."

- Samuel Goldwyn

You have successfully negotiated the best possible terms, right? If you haven't, then you should go back and read Step 6, or review only the sections of Step 6 you are not comfortable with. When you meet again with the seller, you want to be sure you fully understand negotiation terms and are getting the best deal for yourself.

Once you get it in writing, with both you and the seller signing and dating the Purchase Agreement, the IDT (Trust Deed) and the Note, it could be too late to turn back. Of course there is the chance that you both agree to follow any of those documents with written amendments. Don't expect changes you both agree on to happen easily.

This step is the most powerful because it will wrap all the previous steps into a formal package and actually make you the new owner.

Paperwork If You Have an Agent

If you decided to be represented, much of the paperwork will be produced by your Realtor, The format of the documents will be unique to each state or region, although the purpose and structure will generally be the same.

If you are not represented, the following list of documents and their descriptions will help accomplish the same goal.

Paperwork without an Agent

To successfully close the home purchase when you are not represented, you will need to complete at least three of the documents described in this step. The basic set includes between three and ten documents, depending on which forms this book (and each form itself) requires, or suggests for your situation.

The settlement agency, if one is involved as this book recommends, will probably have some, but not all of these forms, as well as additional documents for you and the seller. The forms will be described below.

An important goal here in Step 7 is to help you understand the forms and complete them properly. You will learn which ones to use and in which order.

Here is a list of the primary forms and documents, in order based on a standard transaction timeline:

1.   Purchase Agreement Worksheet

2. Letter of Intent

3. Loan Estimate Worksheet

4. The Purchase Agreement itself

5. Seller Financing Addendum

6. The (Promissory) Note

7. Closing Disclosure

8. Immediate Deed of Trust

9. Deed of Reconveyance

1. The Purchase Agreement Worksheet

You became familiar with this Worksheet in Step 3. You should have completed it during Step 6.

In this Step 7, you will be referring to the entries in the Worksheet to complete the Purchase Agreement.

2. The Letter of Intent

This important letter appears at the end of Step 6. You read about negotiations and then implemented Step 6, but your initial negotiating efforts may have failed.

There are two things you need to do if you have failed to convince the seller to lend to you.

First, if you still hope to buy that house sometime in the near future, provide the seller with the Letter of Intent. Then go back and review Step 6.

If you or the seller have a change of circumstances and you find yourselves agreeing to proceed to a Purchase Agreement, you will need to refer to that existing Letter of Intent. You should have kept a copy of the letter you gave the seller.

3. The Loan Estimate Worksheet

The structure of the CFPB Loan Estimate (LE) form is what you should use as a worksheet to see your loan terms at a glance before committing to the loan itself.

You can find the Loan Estimate Worksheet at:

www.BankFreeHouse.com/Books/Forms

The sample Loan Estimate itself appeared in Step 2.

4. The Purchase Agreement

The seller's signature on this document is your first of two important goals. Once you and the seller have signed it, the Purchase Agreement (PA) is legally binding. Your ultimate goal is to close the purchase. Sounds like a traditional home purchase process, right? So what makes this different?

You already experienced some of the differences during the negotiation process that resulted in the elements that create this PA. With your unique transaction, you should provide a supplemental Seller Financing form, also known as Seller Financing Addendum (see # 5 for details on these forms).

The most important feature of a solid addendum provides a clear focus on the critical differences between a traditional purchase and seller finance. This benefits you, the seller and anyone who needs to scrutinize your transaction in the future.

The next unique aspect of the process will be the handling of the Purchase Agreement by a settlement agency, such as an escrow or a title company. That agency you agree to use should be familiar with creative financing. Ideally they will have performed numerous seller financed transactions (see Appendix C for details about these and other 3rd party providers).

The individual items that appear throughout the PA do not vary greatly, but each U.S. state governing real estate body has its own format. Many states also require a supplemental form for seller financed transactions (see sample supplemental forms from Oklahoma and California).

State recommended Purchase Agreement and supplemental forms can be generic but very similar, created by other third party providers whose business model offers "unofficial" but acceptable forms for sale to the public.

Customers of those forms are usually FSBO sellers (For Sale By Owner). In the less likely event that neither you nor the seller is represented, you will need those unofficial forms. Otherwise, a Realtor will provide them. The settlement agent provides some forms.

Access the full Purchase Agreement at:

www.BankFreeHouse.com/Books/Forms

5. Seller Financing Addendum (CA)

A Seller Financing Addendum should be added to the pages of any Purchase Agreement whenever a seller agrees to extend credit to you as the buyer.

The form in Figure H is the first page of the California Seller Financing Addendum. All similar forms should be as comprehensive, so this is used as an example.

Access the full CA Seller Financing Addendum at:

www.BankFreeHouse.com/Books/Forms

Step 7 - Get It in Writing

CALIFORNIA ASSOCIATION OF REALTORS®

SELLER FINANCING ADDENDUM AND DISCLOSURE
(SEE IMPORTANT DISCLOSURE ON PAGE 4)
(California Civil Code §§2956-2967)
(C.A.R. Form SFA, Revised 11/13)

This is an addendum to the ☒ Residential Purchase Agreement, ☐ Counter Offer, or ☐ Other _____
_____, ("Agreement"), dated _____

On property known as _____ ("Property"),
between _____ ("Buyer"),
and _____ ("Seller").

Seller agrees to extend credit to Buyer as follows:

1. **PRINCIPAL; INTEREST; PAYMENT; MATURITY TERMS:** ☐ Principal amount $ _____ , interest at _____ % per annum,
payable at approximately $ _____ per ☐ month, ☐ year, or ☐ other _____ , remaining principal
balance due in _____ years.

2. **LOAN APPLICATION; CREDIT REPORT:** Within 5 (or _____) Days After Acceptance: (a) Buyer shall provide Seller a completed loan application on a form acceptable to Seller (such as a FNMA/FHLMC Uniform Residential Loan Application for residential one to four unit properties); and (b) Buyer authorizes Seller and/or Agent to obtain, at Buyer's expense, a copy of Buyer's credit report. Buyer shall provide any supporting documentation reasonably requested by Seller. Seller, after first giving Buyer a Notice to Buyer to Perform, may cancel this Agreement in writing and authorize return of Buyer's deposit if Buyer fails to provide such documents within that time, or if Seller disapproves any above item within 5 (or _____) Days After receipt of each item.

3. **CREDIT DOCUMENTS:** This extension of credit by Seller will be evidenced by: ☐ Note and deed of trust; ☐ All-inclusive note and deed of trust; ☐ Installment land sale contract; ☐ Lease/option (when parties intend transfer of equitable title); OR ☐ Other (specify) _____

THE FOLLOWING TERMS APPLY ONLY IF CHECKED. SELLER IS ADVISED TO READ ALL TERMS, EVEN THOSE NOT CHECKED, TO UNDERSTAND WHAT IS OR IS NOT INCLUDED, AND, IF NOT INCLUDED, THE CONSEQUENCES THEREOF.

4. ☐ **LATE CHARGE:** If any payment is not made within _____ Days After it is due, a late charge of either $ _____ , or
_____ % of the installment due, may be charged to Buyer. NOTE: On single family residences that Buyer intends to occupy, California Civil Code §2954.4(a) limits the late charge to no more than 6% of the total installment payment due and requires a grace period of no less than 10 days.

5. ☐ **BALLOON PAYMENT:** The extension of credit will provide for a balloon payment, in the amount of $ _____ , plus any accrued interest, which is due on _____ (date).

6. ☐ **PREPAYMENT:** If all or part of this extension of credit is paid early, Seller may charge a prepayment penalty as follows (if applicable): _____ . Caution: California Civil Code §2954.9 contains limitations on prepayment penalties for residential one-to-four unit properties.

7. ☐ **DUE ON SALE:** If any interest in the Property is sold or otherwise transferred, Seller has the option to require immediate payment of the entire unpaid principal balance, plus any accrued interest.

8. * ☐ **REQUEST FOR COPY OF NOTICE OF DEFAULT:** A request for a copy of Notice of Default as defined in California Civil Code §2924b will be recorded. If not, Seller is advised to consider recording a Request for Notice of Default.

9. * ☐ **REQUEST FOR NOTICE OF DELINQUENCY:** A request for Notice of Delinquency, as defined in California Civil Code §2924e, to be signed and paid for by Buyer, will be made to senior lienholders. If not, Seller is advised to consider making a Request for Notice of Delinquency. Seller is advised to check with senior lienholders to verify whether they will honor this request.

10. ☐ **TAX SERVICE:**
A. If property taxes on the Property become delinquent, tax service will be arranged to report to Seller. If not, Seller is advised to consider retaining a tax service, or to otherwise determine that property taxes are paid.
B. ☐ Buyer, ☐ Seller, shall be responsible for the initial and continued retention of, and payment for, such tax service.

11. ☐ **TITLE INSURANCE:** Title insurance coverage will be provided to both Seller and Buyer, insuring their respective interests in the Property. If not, Buyer and Seller are advised to consider securing such title insurance coverage.

12. ☐ **HAZARD INSURANCE:**
A. The parties' escrow holder or insurance carrier will be directed to include a loss payee endorsement, adding Seller to the Property insurance policy. If not, Seller is advised to secure such an endorsement, or acquire a separate insurance policy.
B. Property insurance does not include earthquake or flood insurance coverage, unless checked:
☐ Earthquake insurance will be obtained; ☐ Flood insurance will be obtained.

13. ☐ **PROCEEDS TO BUYER:** Buyer will receive cash proceeds at the close of the sale transaction. The amount received will be approximately $ _____ , from _____ (indicate source of proceeds). Buyer represents that the purpose of such disbursement is as follows: _____

14. ☐ **NEGATIVE AMORTIZATION; DEFERRED INTEREST:** Negative amortization results when Buyer's periodic payments are less than the amount of interest earned on the obligation. Deferred interest also results when the obligation does not require periodic payments for a period of time. In either case, interest is not payable as it accrues. This accrued interest will have to be paid by Buyer at a later time, and may result in Buyer owing more on the obligation than at its origination. The credit being extended to Buyer by Seller will provide for negative amortization or deferred interest as indicated below. (Check A, B, or C. CHECK ONE ONLY.)
☐ A. All negative amortization or deferred interest shall be added to the principal _____ (e.g., annually, monthly, etc.), and thereafter shall bear interest at the rate specified in the credit documents (compound interest);
OR ☐ B. All deferred interest shall be due and payable, along with principal, at maturity;
OR ☐ C. Other _____

*(For Paragraphs 8-10) In order to receive timely and continued notification, Seller is advised to record appropriate notices and/or to notify appropriate parties of any change in Seller's address.

Buyer's Initials (_____)(_____)   Seller's Initials (_____)(_____)

SFA REVISED 11/13 (PAGE 1 OF 4)   Reviewed by _____ Date _____

SELLER FINANCING ADDENDUM AND DISCLOSURE (SFA PAGE 1 OF 4)

Realty Benefit, 22691 Lambert St. Suite 502 Lake Forest, CA 92618   Phone: 949.290.5348   Fax: 949 597-0440   Untitled
Dean Harris   Produced with zipForm® by zipLogix 18070 Fifteen Mile Road, Fraser, Michigan 48026 www.zipLogix.com

Figure H – The California Seller Finance Addendum

Full descriptions of items in this Addendum follow:

On the California form, the following items # 1 through # 3 must be completed:

1. The basic terms describing the Note can be found in this section.

2. Within 5 days of the acceptance of the Purchase Agreement (or the number of days that both you and the seller agree to) you need to give the completed loan application to the seller.

   You also allow the seller to get a copy of your credit report at your expense.

   Item 2 states that the seller is able to cancel the contract in writing and return your deposit if you don't deliver the completed loan application or the credit report is not available by the deadline.

   The seller must approve each of your submitted documents within 5 days of each receipt.

3. Evidence of the seller's offer of credit must be at least one of the five check box items – Note and deed of trust – AITD – Land Contract – Lease Option – The fifth check box is set aside for an alternate method not previously described.

NOTE: Items after # 3 should be checked or completed only if they apply.

4.   You and the seller may agree to a specific amount as a late charge (or a percent of the monthly payment) after an agreed upon number of days past the due date.

5.   If the agreement includes a balloon payment, the balloon amount and its due date is filled in here.

6.   Complete this entry if you and the seller have agreed to any prepayment penalties.

7.   The seller may exercise the right to collect the entire balance due if you sell or transfer any interest in the property to a third party during the Note term.

8.   After recording, both you and the seller should receive a copy of the Notice of Default, the first step in a foreclosure.

9.   Prior to foreclosure, any late payments can result in a Notice of Delinquency, which would need to be signed and paid for by you.

10.   A)   You and the seller should have agreed to use a third party servicer to manage all payments related to the purchase, including property taxes.

B)   As buyer, you would want the seller to pay for the monthly payments charged by the servicer.

169

11. If you and the seller each want your own title insurance, this would be checked. It is important that you purchase title insurance. The seller may buy a lender's policy.

12. A) Refer to Appendix A – Criticism # 5.

    B) If the house is in an earthquake or flood zone, these policies can pay damage repair. If the house is condemned, they may send you a check to pay for the tear down and rebuild.

13. As an example, the seller may have agreed to give you cash at the close to replace the roof.

14. Sellers should not dare to charge "neg am" or defer payments. Dodd-Frank forbids this but is not yet supported by enough case law. Penalties against sellers will be steep if buyers complain.

6. The Promissory Note

This is the most important document of the group. The Note, when signed by you and the seller, legally binds you to repayment according to its terms.

The first page of "the Note" appears in Figure I (the letter "I" not the number one). The rest of the sample Note can be retrieved at the following URL:

www.BankFreeHouse.com/Books/Forms

Step 7 - Get It in Writing

INSTALLMENT PROMISSORY NOTE

$142,000.00   Date: February 27, 2016

For value received, the undersigned Michael Jones and Mary Stone (the "Borrowers"), at 123 Anywhere Street, Anywhere, ST 12345, promises to pay to the order of Bernard Woods (the "Lender"), at 4321 Random Blvd, Somecity, ST 12340 (or at such other place as the Lender may designate in writing), the sum of $142,000.00 with interest from March 2, 2016, on the unpaid principal at the rate of 5.25% per annum.

I. TERMS OF REPAYMENT

A. Payments. The unpaid principal and accrued interest shall be payable in monthly installments of $784.13, beginning on March 2, 2016, and continuing until March 2, 2023 (the "Due Date"), at which time the remaining unpaid balance shall be due in full.

B. Application of Payments. All payments on this Note shall be applied first in payment of accrued interest and any remainder in payment of principal.

C. Late fees. The Borrower promises to pay a late charge of $35.00 for each installment that remains unpaid more than 21 day(s) after its Due Date. This late charge shall be paid as liquidated damages in lieu of actual damages, and not as a penalty. Payment of such late charge shall, under no circumstances, be construed to cure any default arising from or relating to such late payment.

D. Acceleration of Debt. If any payment obligation under this Note is not paid when due, the remaining unpaid principal balance and any accrued interest shall become due immediately at the option of the Lender.

II. COLLECTION COSTS

If any payment obligation under this Note is not paid when due, the Borrower promises to pay all costs of collection, including reasonable attorney fees, whether or not a lawsuit is commenced as part of the collection process.

III. DEFAULT

If any of the following events of default occur, this Note and any other obligations of the Borrower to the Lender, shall become due immediately, without demand or notice:

A) the failure of the Borrower to pay the principal and any accrued interest when due;

This is a RocketLawyer.com document.

Figure I – Sample Promissory Note ("the Note")

171

7. The Closing Disclosure

The Loan Estimate is the basis for the Closing Disclosure (CD). On the day your loan becomes active, the CD should accurately reflect most all aspects of the agreement with the seller.

Shown here is the sample CD page 1 of 5. You can access the entire CD at the following URL:

www.BankFreeHouse.com/Books/Forms

Figure K – The Closing Disclosure replaces the HUD-1

172

8. The Immediate Deed of Trust (IDT)

When your home ownership document is ready to be recorded, which creative financing document will your local authority accept? They are probably most comfortable working with a state or local form that specifically handles either Pure Seller Financing, "Subject To" or AITD.

Each local area office of each state's Department of Real Estate or Real Estate Commission should have their own form for each of those three types of seller financing.

The Immediate Deed of Trust (IDT) document is a convenient combination of those three well known and common creative sale type documents. The IDT can be used as the Trust Deed serving any one of those contract agreements as well.

The IDT was described in some detail earlier in this book. Refer to item 8 under the section entitled, "8 Ways to Buy a Home without the Bank."

In states where only mortgages are recognized, there is a sample Mortgage Agreement as well.

To find these documents as well as the right office to post your home purchase (the list includes every office in every county in America) visit my website at the following URL:

www.BankFreeHouse.com/Books/Forms

You will find the IDT, the Seller Finance Mortgage Agreement and the Note available for download online. The first page of the

IDT is reprinted below as well. There are other documents for the three creative sale types, but the IDT and the Note comes with instructions. In fact, much of the content is covered in this book, so you should find it easy and convenient.

Some real estate professionals may claim that, because they don't recognize the document, it will not be acceptable to the offices that record the more mainstream deeds of trust. In fact, no recording offices have rejected the IDT to date. All recording offices should accept the IDT.

Most offices have seen many different versions of the three existing types over the past 30 years. Each office will usually scan for the most important paragraphs before accepting it.

If your Realtor can't fully explain some of the IDT terms you might not understand, you should consider getting assistance elsewhere. However, there is a detailed explanation that follows the IDT in this book, so that should help guide you through the completion of this form with a good understanding.

Step 7 - Get It in Writing

IMMEDIATE DEED of TRUST
IDT and Assignment of Rents

This is an Immediate Deed of Trust, made this _____ day of _____ , _____
(Month)   (Year)

between _____ herein called TRUSTOR, whose address is
(Insert Trustor's Name)

_____   _____   _____   _____
(Number and Street)   (City)   (State)   (Zip)

and _____ , herein called TRUSTEE, and _____
(Insert Trustee's Name)   (Insert Lender's Name)

herein called BENEFICIARY.

WITNESSETH:

That Trustor IRREVOCABLY GRANTS, TRANSFERS and ASSIGNS to TRUSTEE IN

TRUST, WITH POWER OF SALE, that property in _____ County, _____
(State)

described as:_____
(The Legal Description)
_____

TOGETHER WITH the rents, issues and profits thereof, SUBJECT, HOWEVER, to the
right, power and authority hereinafter given to and conferred upon Beneficiary to collect
and apply such rents, issues and profits.

For the Purpose of Securing:

1. Performance of each agreement of Trustor herein contained.

2. Payment of the indebtedness evidenced by the original purchase money
   promissory note (the "Note") with a maturity year of _____
   herewith, and any extension or renewal thereof, in the principal sum of
   $ _____ executed by Trustor in favor of Beneficiary.

Underlying Obligations:

This Immediate Deed of Trust includes and secures additional purchase money
obligations in the principal amount of $_____ which includes within the
amount the unpaid balance of the following:

1. A promissory note in favor of _____ as Payee, secured by a
   (Name of Beneficiary)

   Deed of Trust recorded _____ as Document No. _____
   (Date of Recording)   (Instrument No.)

   in Book ____ , Page ____ , in the Official Records of _____County, _____
   (State)

Figure J – The IDT (Immediate Deed of Trust)

All 8 pages at www.BankFreeHouse.com/Books/Forms

Buy a House with No Bank Loan   Dean Harris

The Homebuyer's Guide to Filling Out the Immediate Deed of Trust (IDT)

Before you begin working on this document, check to be sure the government authorities will recognize Trust Deeds where the house described in item 3 is located. If the authorities only recognize mortgages, you may seller finance but you can't use the IDT.

As is the case with a mortgage, the IDT identifies the house as collateral for the loan in case the Buyer defaults on payments to the Seller. The IDT does not replace the Note as a detailed description of the loan terms. It does pledge the house as collateral if the buyer stops paying. The terms of the loan must be described in detail in the (Promissory) Note before completing this IDT form.

The Buyer must have already agreed to be obligated to repay a specific loan amount to the Seller based on the terms described in the Note. If more than one loan currently exists on the house, this total loan amount will represent a consolidation of all of the currently outstanding loan balances.

Each of the underlying Notes should have already been properly recorded at the local government office.

If the Note was secured by a Mortgage, then the lender has the legal right to foreclose, but only through the court system.

If the Note was secured by a Trust Deed then "Bare" legal title to the house remains with the Trustee until the Note is paid in full. This means the Trustee is limited to the legal right to foreclose, but only if the buyer stops making payments and the Beneficiary directs the Trustee to foreclose. With a trust deed, foreclosure does not involve the court system.

Whether the home loan was secured with a mortgage or a trust deed, the Buyer has "full" legal title at the close and until the loan is fully paid, foreclosed, transferred or assumed, if assumption was an option.

With a trust deed, when the Buyer pays the entire loan, he or she must complete the Deed of Reconveyance, get it notarized and have it recorded at the County Recorder's Office. This type of deed removes the Trustee's position, which means the Trustee no longer has the power to foreclose.

When the home is secured by a mortgage and the Buyer pays the entire home loan, he or she must complete a Satisfaction of Mortgage, get it notarized and have it recorded at the County Recorder's Office.

The IDT, as well as the written guide for completing the IDT can be found at

www.BankFreeHouse.com/Books/Forms

9. Grant Deed

The grant deed is usually the last paperwork in the process. The sample grant deed you find in the online forms library reflects the sample seller financed purchase by the same buyer couple you have seen in the other sample forms.

www.BankFreeHouse.com/Books/Forms

Appendix A - **How to Handle IDT Critics**

Buyers should expect to deal with co-workers, friends and even family members who believe they know the reasons why these home buying methods are not legitimate or won't work. Co-workers, friends and family members don't base their opinions on reality, because the fact is thousands of happy and successful homeowners who otherwise would not have been able to buy have bought homes this way. Buyers are not the only happy folks. The sellers have also been very satisfied.

This myth busting appendix should help calm any fears you may have about buying this way. After reading these entries, use this section as a reference whenever you encounter an objection before, during or after your transaction.

Criticism # 1
No Seller Would Agree to This

False - Sellers in past sales have clearly understood and benefited greatly from agreeing to finance their buyers. If today's sellers knew exactly how many of those sellers' lives have been improved, they would also offer to finance their buyers. For today's sellers who cling to the belief that it's critically important to receive the entire purchase price immediately, refer to Figure 5 – How much more the seller will make by lending to the buyer.

What is another important reason sellers agree to this? The seller does NOT become a landlord. This is not a lease and tenant situation. The seller does no maintenance and pays no property taxes or insurance. What does happen is that the seller can expect a check in the mail every month.

Why can they expect a check every month during their agreement? If the buyer defaults, the seller can legally keep the buyer's down payment and all payments made before that. The buyer loses the house to foreclosure and the seller can sell the house to the next buyer. Do buyers want that? Of course not! From the seller's point of view, that's a low risk, high return investment and that's why they sleep so well.

Sellers who are experiencing financial difficulties will gladly give up legal ownership of their home while keeping their name on the home loan. Many sellers in a financial bind need to be told this option exists!

In other cases, more and more sellers see the financial benefits associated with receiving monthly checks in excess of the amount owed. In fact, the receipt of monthly income is especially smart for sellers who have no existing loans on their seller financed home. Refer to Section E for a description of the three types of sellers who are likely to offer financing and the reasons why.

Criticism # 2
This Type of Transaction is Illegal

False - It's difficult to believe that anyone still believes that such a well-known, widely used method of home purchase for decades is somehow against the law. Even the new rules under the Dodd-Frank Act continue to support seller finance (see Criticism #6).

The U.S. Department of Housing and Urban Development (HUD) has always recognized that sellers can legally extend credit directly to buyers.

The proof appears on the first page of the three page HUD-1 form (shown in Figure 6) which had been used as a U.S. "settlement" form nationwide until October 3, 2015. On the HUD1 form under seller's Section K, item 503 you can see that item is labeled, "Existing Loan(s) Taken Subject To."
On the new "Closing Disclosure" (CD) form that replaces the HUD-1, the same label appears on Section L. You can find that entry in Section L on page 3 of 5.

This covers "Subject To" as well as AITD type transactions. It does not cover Pure Seller Financing because no bank or lending institution is involved in a transaction without a pre-existing loan. The HUD-1 form or the CD would not be necessary in that case.

As additional evidence of the widespread acceptance of the legitimacy of seller financing, most U.S. State agencies regulating real estate transactions include separate and specific forms used exclusively for those types of transactions.

The State agencies require their Settlement firms and State licensed agents and brokers to use these forms whenever their client transaction involves the lending of seller equity. Again, such a transaction would include one of two seller financing types – "Subject To," and the AITD."

Figure 7 is taken from Oklahoma's public records and Figure 8 is taken from Utah's public records.

180

Appendix A - How to Handle IDT Critics

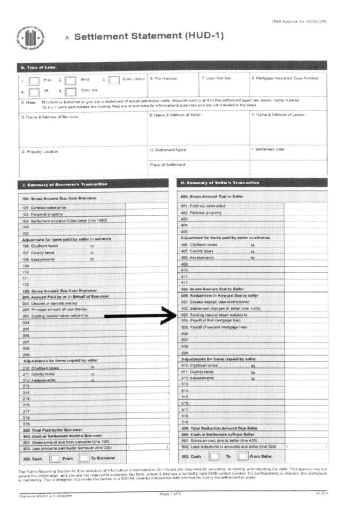

Figure 6 – The HUD-1 Settlement Statement

Appendix A - How to Handle IDT Critics

OKLAHOMA REAL ESTATE COMMISSION
This is a legally binding Contract; if not understood, seek advice from an attorney.

SELLER FINANCING

This financing supplement, which is attached to and part of the Oklahoma Uniform Contract of Sale of Real Estate relates to the following described real estate:

_____

(Check Applicable)

☐ **Mortgage Carried by Seller (Amortized)**
The balance of the purchase price shall be paid in the following manner: At Closing, Buyer shall execute a negotiable promissory note payable to the order of Seller in the sum of $_____, payable in _____ equal monthly installments of $_____, including principal and interest, beginning on the _____ day of _____, 20____ and continuing on the _____ day of each month thereafter with interest at the rate of _____ percent (%) per annum on the unpaid balance.

☐ **Mortgage Carried by Seller (One Payment)**
The balance of the purchase price shall be paid in the following manner: At Closing, Buyer shall execute a negotiable promissory note payable to the order of Seller in the sum of $_____, due and payable on _____, 20____ with interest at the rate of _____ percent (%) per annum.

☐ **Mortgage Carried by Seller Amortized With Balloon Payment**
The balance of the purchase price shall be paid in the following manner: At Closing, Buyer shall execute a negotiable promissory note payable to the order of Seller in the sum of $_____, payable in _____ equal monthly installments of $_____, including principal and interest, beginning on the _____ day of _____, 20____ continuing on the _____ day of each month thereafter with an interest rate of _____ percent (%) per annum on the unpaid balance. Said note shall be amortized over _____ months with the entire unpaid principal balance (Balloon payment) to be paid in full as the _____ payment.

The Mortgage Documents carried by Seller shall include, but not be limited to, the following provisions:

  i)   prepayment at any time without penalty
  ii) acceleration of the balance due upon the transfer of the title to the Property to any third party
  iii) the delivery of a _____ mortgage on the Property as security
  iv) the promissory note shall be personally guaranteed by _____
  v)   the mortgage shall contain the following partial release provision(s): _____
       _____

  vi) additional provision(s): _____

The remainder of the purchase price shall be paid in cash at Closing.

The note and mortgage to be furnished by Seller and delivered to Buyer not later than _____ days (ten [10] days if left blank), prior to Closing. The expense of preparing these documents shall be paid by_____, not to exceed a total of $_____.

Buyer's Signature	Date	Seller's Signature	Date
Buyer's Signature	Date	Seller's Signature	Date

This form was created by the Oklahoma Real Estate Contract Form Committee and approved by the Oklahoma Real Estate Commission.
OREC SELLER FINANCING (11-2011)   Page 1 of 1

Figure 7 – The Oklahoma Real Estate Commission Seller Financing Contract

WHEN RECORDED MAIL TO:

_____

_____

_____

SPACE ABOVE THIS LINE FOR RECORDER

All-Inclusive Trust Deed

With Assignment of Rents

THIS ALL-INCLUSIVE TRUST DEED made this .... day of _____ 19 ____ between _____

_____ as TRUSTOR,

whose address is _____

     (Street and Number)   (City)   (State)

_____, as TRUSTEE,* and

_____, as BENEFICIARY,

WITNESSETH: That Trustor CONVEYS AND WARRANTS TO TRUSTEE IN TRUST, WITH POWER OF SALE, the following described property
situated in _____ County, State of Utah.

Together with all buildings, fixtures and improvements thereon and all water rights, rights of way, easements, rents, and issues, profits, income
tenements, hereditaments, privileges and appurtenances hereunto belonging, now or hereafter used or enjoyed with said property, or any part thereof,
SUBJECT, HOWEVER, to the right, power and authority hereinafter given to and conferred upon Beneficiary to collect and apply such rents, issues, and
profits;

FOR THE PURPOSE OF SECURING (1) payment of the indebtedness evidenced by an All-Inclusive Promissory Note (hereinafter the "Note") of
even date herewith, in the principal sum of $ _____, made by Trustor, payable to the order of Beneficiary at the times, in the manner
and with interest as therein set forth, and any extensions and/or renewals or modifications thereof; (2) the performance of each agreement of Trustor
herein contained; (3) the payment of such additional loans or advances as hereafter may be made to Trustor, or his successors or assigns, when
evidenced by a Promissory Note or Notes reciting that they are secured by this Trust Deed; and (4) the payment of all sums expended or advanced by
Beneficiary under or pursuant to the terms hereof, together with interest thereon as herein provided.

This instrument is an All-Inclusive Trust Deed subject and subordinate to the following instruments (hereinafter "Senior Encumbrances"):

(1) A Trust Deed/Mortgage recorded _____, as Entry No. _____ in Book _____ at Page _____ of
Official Records of _____, which, if a Trust Deed secures a Promissory Note
in the original principal amount of, or if a Mortgage, is in the original principal amount of _____
Dollars. ($ _____), dated _____ 19 _____, in favor of _____
Beneficiary/Mortgagee, with the Trustor/Mortgagor being _____
If a Trust Deed, its Trustee is _____

(2) A Trust Deed/Mortgage recorded _____, as Entry No. _____ in Book _____ at Page _____ of
Official Records of _____, which, if a Trust Deed secures a Promissory Note
in the original principal amount of, or if a Mortgage, is in the original principal amount of _____
Dollars. ($ _____), dated _____ 19 _____, in favor of _____
Beneficiary/Mortgagee, with the Trustor/Mortgagor being _____
If a Trust Deed, its Trustee is _____

The Promissory Note(s) secured by said Trust Deed(s) is (are) hereinafter referred to as the "Senior Note(s)"). Nothing in this Trust Deed, the Note,
or any deed in connection herewith shall be deemed to be an assumption by the Trustor of the Senior Notes or Senior Encumbrances.

*NOTE: Trustee must be a member of the Utah State Bar, a bank, building and loan association, savings and loan association, or insurance company
authorized to do such business in Utah; a corporation authorized to conduct a trust business in Utah; a title insurance or abstract company authorized
to do such business in Utah, or a U.S. Government Agency.

This form has been approved by the Utah Real Estate Commission.

Figure 8 – The Utah State Recommended AITD Form – The Deed of Trust Itself

183

Criticism # 3
The "Due on Sale" Clause Will be Triggered

In many cases the house you want to buy will already have a bank loan in the seller's name.

The criticism you will hear most often is the threat that banks will demand immediate payment in full if they discover that a transfer of ownership has taken place. Your response to this warning is as follows:

In the real world, banks do not start a collection effort of any kind unless the home loan payments are seriously overdue. They do not want the time, expense and aggravation of collections, especially when the payments have been arriving on a timely basis In fact, if banks did start an action, they know they would risk the future receipt of those precious timely payments. What is worse, the banks would have no guarantee they would ever see another penny!

The Due on Sale clause is part of the Garn Act that was passed in 1982. Although it is technically still in effect, Due on Sale demands have been as rare as legitimate sightings of Bigfoot or the Loch Ness monster, in part for the reasons listed above. If collection activity does take place while you own the house, it would be the result of foreclosure, not the Due on Sale clause.

As a buyer, there are three powerful protections you can provide for yourself.

1. The day you bought the house, you should have agreed to have a reputable third party servicer whose responsibility,

among several, is to let you know on a monthly basis that the seller is paying the bank on time (see Criticism #4).

2. If you simply avoid being late on payments to the seller, you avoid any type of collection activity. You also build yourself a higher credit score.

3. Although you do not get legal title until the loan is paid in full, when a Land Trust is created, the bank is not notified about a change of ownership.

Recording the Beneficial Interest in the Trust is not required. Therefore, the change of ownership naming you as the buyer and new homeowner is not disclosed. The change is very difficult to research and discover.

Criticism # 4
The Seller May Stop Paying the Bank

This situation can happen but it's very rare. In the past, a seller had been able to get greedy or forgetful.

What makes it greedy? The seller used to be able to take the house back in foreclosure relatively easily. Many years ago, the seller could then keep your down payment and all the payments you have made as well. The seller was too easily able to willfully resell the house to the next buyer for even more profit.

There is the possibility that the seller would honestly forget to pay. But if the seller gets into financial trouble, then deliberately withholding the payments until the bank begins collection attempts is another possibility. The bank sometimes takes the next step and issues a default notice, the first step in a foreclosure.

In some cases the house is lost without notice to the buyer and through no fault of the buyer, although the seller had been aware. Here is your response to this warning:

You arc going to avoid any such problem by joining the many smart seller financed buyers who learned from those past mistakes. As mentioned in Item Number 1 in Criticism Number 3, you are going to insist on having a reliable, experienced third party management firm with a good reputation, such as Evergreen Notes, monitor, collect and send monthly house payment invoices, receipts and reports to both you and the seller during the entire term of your loan.

Criticism # 5
The Insurance Company May Deny Claims

It can be argued that, in the event of an insurance claim, the insurance company may deny coverage based on the seller's transfer of ownership to you. It has been true that claims in these situations have often been denied.

There are at least three proven solutions to this otherwise serious problem. But it requires that both you and the seller be proactive. Carefully consider the consequences and take one of those actions before signing the Purchase Agreement and Note.

Find the written solutions online at
www.BankFreeHouse.com/Books/Forms

Criticism # 6
The Dodd-Frank Act Makes This Illegal

Seller financing is NOT illegal under the Dodd-Frank Act. Seller financing continues to be recognized as legal, but with a few new guidelines.

As an example, it wasn't long ago that home sellers who offered to be your lender were under no legal obligation to be sure your interest rate was tied to a specific index. Nor did the rate have to be in place for a minimum of 5 years with a 2 percent ceiling on annual rate increases and a lifetime maximum of 6 percent above the original interest rate.

In fact, if the seller does only one seller financed transaction in a year, that transaction is still allowed to include a balloon payment. However, if this is not your seller's first seller financed transaction this year, a balloon payment cannot be part of your Note.

If your seller has already done five seller financed transactions this year, then a licensed NMLS loan originator is needed to complete your transaction.

According to the section of Dodd-Frank called Ability to Repay, the seller will NOT be required to review or document your finances if he or she has seller financed fewer than 6 houses in a 12 month period. Even so, you should be aware that sellers are generally advised to research every buyer's ability to repay for that house and any other house that the seller owns that he or she has seller financed.

187

So this does not mean that your seller will not review your finances. It only means that the seller is not required to comply with the law by securing copies of your financial documents. The seller may want those documents anyway.

For those interested in how and why the game has changed, here is some information about the new laws.

In July 2013, Congress passed the "Ability to Repay" that supplemented the existing Dodd-Frank Act requirements and spelled out creditor legal obligations. The ATR took effect on January 10, 2014.

In the unlikely event that your seller has financed more than 5 houses this past year, you, the buyer, will need to give the seller copies of much of your financial paperwork. Be aware that your seller must, by law, cover the following eight categories for financial verification of your ability to pay the loan:

The CFPB stated that an annual interest rate increase of two percentage points or less is reasonable, and a reasonable lifetime limitation would be an increase of 6 percent or less.

If sellers do not qualify for one of the seller financing exclusions above, they may need to abandon their plan to finance the sale of their own property. Buyers who still want that seller's house must work with a licensed loan originator, a bank or other lending institution or entity to get financing.

Most sellers are exempt and will carry the loan on only one house in any 12 month period, even if they own other homes.

Appendix B – **Real Estate Terms Defined**

Glossary

Ability to Repay - (see also "Dodd-Frank Act")

This section 129C of the legislation known as the Dodd-Frank Act took effect on January 10, 2014.

The Ability to Repay (ATR) requires that some sellers who offer to finance their house must secure reasonable written proof that the buyer can afford to make payments until the loan is paid in full. Sellers who have financed fewer than six houses in a calendar year are exempt.

Acceleration Clause (see also "Due on Sale")

Single or multiple paragraphs used in an installment note which gives the lender the right to demand payment in full if certain events described in the clause take place.

Destruction of the property is one such event. Change of ownership without the lender's consent is another such event although consistent and timely loan payments make the use of this draconian penalty highly unlikely.

Adjustable Rate Mortgage (ARM)

Home loans in which the interest rate is periodically adjusted to more closely coincide with current rates. The amounts and times of adjustment are agreed to at the inception of the loan.

AITD (acronym for "All Inclusive Trust Deed")

This is one of the three loan types associated with an IDT ("Immediate Deed of Trust"). The AITD is also referred to as a "Wrap-Around Mortgage" or simply a "Wrap." The buyer is expected to make scheduled payments to the seller for the new single loan that includes all other loans on that property including the new loan that the seller lends against his or her equity.

The seller then makes the pre-existing scheduled monthly loan payments, usually to a bank, and keeps the additional cash from the equity loan as profit.

Amortization

It is the payment of a debt in equal installments of principal and interest that gradually reduces the principal balance.

An interest only payment does not amortize the debt. Amortization of an Adjustable Rate Mortgage (ARM) will not feature equal installments of principal and interest when the loan adjusts or is recast.

If the loan features a balloon payment in which the final payment is a large balance that usually results in a refinance, the loan is not considered fully amortized.

Annual Percentage Rate (also "APR")

The APR includes both the nominal interest rate and the charges for borrowing.

Like the nominal interest rate, the APR is expressed as a percentage. Unlike the nominal interest rate, the APR represents the actual yearly charges, including the interest rate, spread out over the term of the loan.

Appraisal

The formal evaluation of a home property value based on factual analysis and performed by at least one licensed residential appraiser.

In the absence of a licensed appraiser, other types of (less formal) appraisals include automated and BPO known as a Broker Price Opinion.

Assignment of Rents

In the event the borrower stops paying the Note, the buyer/borrower agrees to surrender the right to continue receiving tenant rental income, if any exists. The seller/lender then has the right to begin collecting that income.

Assumed Loan (See also "Loan Assumption")

The lender agrees to have a buyer other than the original buyer take over the liability under an existing note. The lender must approve the new debtor in order to release the existing debtor from liability.

Back End Ratio

A ratio that indicates what portion of a person's monthly income goes toward paying debts.

Total monthly debt includes expenses such as home loan payments (see also PITI), credit card payments, child support and other loan payments. Banks and institutional lenders use this ratio in conjunction with the front end ratio to approve home loans.

Balloon Payment

This kind of payment is the result of a Note that calls for periodic payments which are insufficient to fully amortize the face amount of the Note prior to maturity. The balloon payment is the remaining principal sum which is due in full at maturity.

Beneficiary

In this book, the "beneficiary" is the seller who benefits from the monthly profit and has the ability to repossess the house if the borrower stops paying the seller financed Note.

BPO (acronym for "Broker Price Opinion")

A BPO is a less formal appraisal that is not performed by a licensed appraiser. Instead, the BPO is performed by a licensed real estate broker or agent.

Buyer's Market (See also "Seller's Market")

A buyer's market exists when there are more houses for sale than there are buyers. In such a market, buyers generally have the upper hand in negotiations. History has shown that seller's markets are more common.

Carry Paper

The "paper" is the Note, which is the short version of the Promissory Note. When the seller agrees to become the lender, the seller is said to "carry." The seller is also said to "carry paper" or "carry the Note."

Corporate (Warranty) Deed (see also "Deeds")

This is one of several special types of a warranty deed in which the buyer or seller is a legal entity, but not necessarily a corporation. This is more common in commercial real estate and can apply to large condo complexes. Warranty deeds have become less popular since title companies have been more widely accepted as the guarantors of title through insurance.

Closing (a.k.a. "The Close" or "The Closing")

The day your house purchase becomes final.

Closing Costs

On the day your house purchase becomes final, these are expenses to be paid as previously agreed between you and the seller. Seller financing closing costs are almost always far lower than those associated with a bank loan.

Counter Offer

An offer made in response to a previous offer by the other party during negotiations. The act of making a counter offer means the prior offer is rejected. If the counter offer is not accepted, there is no contract.

Credit (see also "FICO")

One seller financing definition of credit is the seller's level of confidence in the buyer's ability to pay in the future for that which the buyer receives today.

For housing, credit covers more than just the amount of the home loan the buyer qualifies for. Tight credit means qualifying is more difficult.

The term credit also includes the minimum credit scores required by each lender. When credit is tight, higher scores are almost always required.

Debt to Income (DTI)

A lending term that describes the hopeful borrower's monthly debt compared to his or her monthly gross income. Most lenders use Debt to Income to determine whether a home loan applicant would be able to maintain payments on a specific property for the foreseeable future.

Deeds

Ownership, or the release of ownership of a house, is evidenced by several types of deeds. The deeds can be **corporation** deeds, **grant** deeds, **quitclaim** deeds, **warranty** deeds and special types of warranty deeds.

A **Quitclaim Deed** is evidence of a release of ownership. All prove that a conveyance took place.

The **Performance Deed of Trust** is a type of deed used to secure contract obligations other than, or in addition to, the payment of money. The other obligations require the Grantor, who may also be a borrower in this Deed, to perform legal or repair work to satisfy the lien created by this Deed.

The **Revocable Transfer on Death Deed** (RTDD) allows the homeowner to designate a beneficiary in the event of the homeowner's death. After the homeowner dies, the RTDD becomes irrevocable and the beneficiary can take legal ownership without the need for probate.

This is the same benefit that a Living Trust allows. However, the Living Trust offers far more protection from probate than just the house. Prior to the homeowner's death, the RTDD lets the homeowner change or remove the beneficiary (or invalidate the RTDD) at any time without any requirement of notice to the beneficiary.

The **Deed of Trust** is an exception because it is the only type of deed that does not indicate ownership as its primary function. Also known as the **Trust Deed,** it is a security instrument that identifies the house as collateral for the Note. A Trust Deed is a security instrument used in non-judicial states. A Mortgage is the security instrument used in judicial states.

Distressed Property

Real property that has seen its market price reduced because of owner or external misfortunes, such as intense weather, threatened foreclosure, divorce, vandalism or other adverse legal actions.

Dodd-Frank Act (see also "Ability to Repay")

This 2010 legislation created oversight for many aspects of the financial markets, primarily the mortgage loan industry. These new government regulations were intended to prevent a recurrence of the financial crisis of 2008 caused largely by the housing bubble that preceded the crisis. The Dodd-Frank Act's effect on seller financing is outlined in Appendix A.

Down Payment

The amount the buyer pays to reduce the total amount of the home loan before making the first loan payment.

Due on Sale (see also "Acceleration Clause")

Single or multiple paragraphs used in an installment note which gives the lender the right to demand payment in full if certain events described in the clause actually take place.

Destruction of the property is one such event. Change of ownership without the lender's consent is another, although timely and uninterrupted payments make this enforcement method highly unlikely. Due on Sale has rarely been imposed.

Earnest Money Deposit

Shortly after signing a real estate purchase contract, this is the buyer's upfront deposit made to show serious intent to purchase the seller's real property. The deposit amount is generally between 1% and 3% of the purchase price. When the transaction is finalized at the closing table, the deposit becomes part of the down payment.

Equitable Title (see also "Legal Title")

An equitable titleholder has the eventual right to full legal ownership pending satisfaction of agreed upon terms with the legal titleholder. The person with equitable title may live in the

197

property but cannot transfer the property to another party. Equitable titleholders can also benefit by retaining all of the property's appreciation, if any, from the start of the agreement through the end of the agreement.

In a Land Trust, for example, the person named as "Beneficial Interest" holds equitable title.

FICO (see also "Credit")

This is an acronym for the company that created this scoring system. Fair, Isaac and Company was founded by William Fair and Earl Isaac in 1956. Since then, three credit firms (Equifax, Trans Union and Experian) have dominated the reporting aspect while the FICO scoring system has been used by all three firms.

Each firm has always produced slight variations in their scoring models, so there are usually three slightly different scores for each of the three reports. Most lenders settle on the "middle" firm's FICO score. In 2006, the 3 credit firms released their own **Vantage** score system. To date, Vantage has not had the kind of acceptance that FICO has had.

Front End Ratio

A ratio that indicates what portion of a person's monthly income is used to make home loan payments. It is calculated as an individual's monthly housing expenses divided by his or her monthly gross income and is expressed as a percentage. Banks and institutional lenders use the front end ratio in conjunction with the back end ratio to approve loans.

Future Value ("FV")

A formula that solves for the value of an asset at a date in the future that is based on that asset's value today.

Grant Deed

This document gives title to real property from one party (grantor) to another (grantee) when the property has no loans associated with it. Grant deed is a common method of conveyance of ownership in certain states and areas. Trust deeds are not methods of conveyance. Trust deeds are issued as security instruments that document the property as collateral for the loan.

IDT (acronym for the Immediate Deed of Trust)

This document can be used for each of three distinct types of seller financing which include "Pure" seller financing, "Subject To" and "AITD." Upon completion, including signatures from the home buyer and seller, this document becomes a binding security instrument. The "Note" is a separate instrument that provides the terms of the home loan.

Interest Rate

The cost of borrowing money, expressed as a percentage of the loan amount.

Judicial (see also "Non-Judicial")

Judicial describes the administration of justice and the rules of law that depend on the court system.

Over the past decade, the majority of U.S. states have begun realizing the need to eliminate the expensive backlogs caused by lengthy real estate related court procedures typical of the judicial system. This is why these states have been adopting the more efficient real estate procedures that exist under the Non-Judicial system.

Legal Title (see also "Equitable Title")

The rights associated with the recorded document that bears the name of the legal owner, including the right to the possession of the specified real property, as well as the right to enforce debt collection such as foreclosure against any person or entity with an equitable interest in that property who has been late or has missed payments.

Loan Assumption (See also "Assumed Loan")

The lender agrees to have a buyer other than the original buyer take over the liability under an existing note. The lender must approve the new debtor in order to release the existing debtor from liability.

Loan Term (See also "Loan Terms")

Loan term is not the same as the loan "terms." When term is singular, it refers only to the entire length of the loan agreement, expressed in years.

Loan Terms (See also "Loan Term")

"Loan terms" is not the same as the loan "term."
When term is plural as it is here, it refers to the many different items within the loan agreement, known collectively as the Promissory Note.

LTV (acronym for Loan to Value)

The ratio LTV is a percentage of the amount of the loan to the value of the real property. In most cases, especially with bank loans, the higher the percentage, the higher the interest rate charged. If the LTV is too high, the buyer can too easily walk away from the house and the loan. Most banks and institutional lenders will not offer financing if the LTV is too high.

MIP (see also "Mortgage Insurance" and "PMI")

When the borrower is unable to offer a down payment of at least 20 percent, FHA loans require that the borrower pay mortgage insurance premiums (MIP).

Mortgage (see also "Deeds" and "Note")

Used only in judicial states and regions, a mortgage is a document that identifies the house as collateral for the Note. In non-judicial states and regions, a mortgage is replaced by a trust deed, a.k.a. deed of trust. Whether the document is a mortgage or a trust deed, it gives the lender the right to foreclose if the borrower stops paying the Note.

Mortgage Insurance (see "PMI" and "MIP")

When the borrower is unable to offer a down payment of at least 20 percent, certain types of loans will require a monthly premium known as mortgage insurance. The premiums protect the lender against the risk of borrower default that is often the side effect of a low down payment.

Conventional mortgages have Private Mortgage Insurance (PMI). FHA loans have the borrower pay Mortgage Insurance Premiums (MIP). They are two different names for the same type of loan insurance.

Non-Judicial (see also "Judicial")

This is the method that replaces the court system with a less formal process to achieve the same or similar results more efficiently. Over the past decade, the majority of U.S. states have begun realizing the need to eliminate the expensive backlogs caused by lengthy real estate related court procedures typical of the judicial system.

202

Saving time and money is why these states have been adopting the more efficient procedures under the Non-Judicial system.

There are still states that are not entirely willing to give up the judicial system. Some of those states have compromised by allowing certain areas within the state to offer Non-Judicial transactions (see the charts defining judicial and non-judicial in Appendix D)

Non-Performing Note

The generally accepted definition: (Promissory) Note that features a borrower who has missed one payment or was at least 3 months late with any payment. This can seriously decrease the value of the Note, if or when the seller attempts to sell it.

Non-Recourse (see also "Recourse")

If the collateral value of the home of the defaulting buyer is not high enough to satisfy the outstanding balance of the loan, the lender can seize the home but is unable to legally seek repayment of the balance from the buyer.

Note – "the Note" (see also "Promissory Note")

This is a contract spelling out the terms of a promise by one person to pay a sum of money to another, usually in exchange for real property. In this book, the Note involves the person selling the house as the lender and the buyer as the borrower. Among other provisions, the terms include the principal amount owed, the interest rate and the maturity date. (see Sample Note)

Performance Deed of Trust

A Deed of Trust used to secure contract obligations other than, or in addition to, the payment of money. The other obligations require the Grantor, who may also be the borrower in this Deed, to perform legal, repair or maintenance work to satisfy the lien created by this Deed. Sellers have sometimes enforced this type of Trust in a civil court and not foreclosure.

Performing Note

The generally accepted definition: (Promissory) Note that features a borrower, who is current on the payments, has never missed a payment or may have been late once or twice but was less than 3 months late. This kind of good record helps maintain the value of the Note, if or when the seller attempts to sell the Note.

PMI (see also "Mortgage Insurance" and "MIP")

Conventional mortgages require private mortgage insurance (PMI) if the borrower is unable to offer a down payment of at least 20 percent.

Points

On a bank loan, each "point" represents a paid reduction in the buyer's interest rate. One point usually reduces the rate between one-eighth and one-quarter of a percent

The cost of one point is one percent of the purchase price of the house. For example, if you are expected to pay 2 points on a loan of $200,000, that would be 2 percent of the loan amount, or $4,000. This charge is usually expected to be paid in a lump sum at the closing table.

Prepaids

Lenders often require buyers to make advance payments at the loan closing. The payments are made on items such as interest, property taxes and homeowner's insurance.

These expenses represent funding of an escrow (impound) account that the lender uses to pay property taxes and insurance.

Principal, Interest, Taxes & Insurance (PITI)

All of the component parts of a complete home loan payment, including property taxes, homeowners insurance and mortgage insurance (if applicable). An "interest only" payment is not PITI. Principal and interest" payments are not PITI either.

Promissory Note (see also "Note")

This document is most often referred to simply as the "Note." The Note is sometimes confused with the "mortgage" or the "deed of trust" which pledges the property as collateral. The Note does not pledge the property as collateral.

Proration (also "prorated")

The process that fairly divides property expenses between the buyer and seller so that each party only pays for the days that the property is owned.

Pure Seller Financing

This term applies when a seller with no existing loans on the property agrees to use the seller's equity to lend to a buyer that allows that buyer to purchase the seller's property.

Quitclaim Deed

Instead of conveying ownership, an owner who signs this type of deed relinquishes ownership of the property described.

Reconveyance

The transfer of real property that takes place when a home loan is fully paid and the owner is free from the former debt.

The former Borrower, the Trustor on the Deed of Trust, now becomes the legal owner on the document that is known as the Deed of Reconveyance.

Recourse (see also "Non-Recourse")

This is a type of loan secured by collateral, which is usually real property. If the borrower defaults, the lender can seize the collateral with an added benefit.

If the collateral value is not high enough to satisfy the outstanding balance, the lender is able to legally seek cash repayment of the balance directly from the buyer at some point in the future.

Recurring Costs (also "recurring debt")

These are regularly occurring costs, the time frame and frequency of which are described in one or more contract(s) the home buyer agrees to. Three examples of this kind of debt are property taxes, association dues and home insurance.

Refinance

A refinance is a new loan, usually from a bank or other institutional lender that pays off an existing loan on the same property with the same borrower, and sometimes with the same lender as well

Revocable Transfer on Death Deed (RTDD)

This document allows the homeowner to designate a beneficiary in the event of the homeowner's death. After the homeowner dies, the RTDD becomes irrevocable and the beneficiary can take legal ownership without the need for probate. This is the same benefit that a Living Trust allows. However, the Living Trust offers more protection from probate than just the house.

Subject To

This is one of the three seller finance loan types associated with an IDT ("Immediate Deed of Trust"). The seller offers to transfer ownership but agrees to continue to be the named borrower on the existing loan. The buyer's new role as borrower is "subject to" (inherits) the existing payments on the loan(s) as well as takes responsibility for any existing liens.

Sweat Equity

This allows the buyer to do work on the property in exchange for all or part of the down payment or other expenses of the purchase - often closing costs.

Title

Title describes the right to the possession of property, especially real property. This includes the documentary evidence of such right that is generally recorded in a local government office.

(See also the definitions of "legal" and "equitable" title)

Trust Deed (see also "Deed of Trust")

An exception to other deed types, because it is the only type of deed that does not indicate ownership. Its function is a security instrument that identifies the house as collateral for the Note.

Trustee

An individual or entity appointed, or required by law, to execute a trust. A trustee can also hold title to real property under a deed of trust.

Trustor

An individual or organization that gifts funds or assets to others by transferring fiduciary duty to a third party trustee that will maintain the assets for the benefit of one or more of the beneficiaries.

Warranty Deed

By issuing this deed, the seller personally guarantees the title is clear. Title insurance renders this useless.

209

Appendix C – Third Party Services

Third Party Services

USE THE FOLLOWING NAMED SERVICES TO IMPROVE THE
QUALITY AND INTEGRITY OF YOUR HOUSE PURCHASE.

To best serve both you and the seller, you should partner with
service organizations that have been in business for many years
and have a reputation for adding value to home sales as well as
this particular kind of sale.

This section includes links to, and descriptions of title, escrow,
attorney, home inspector and other firms. They will be a great
help to both you and the seller.

Many of these firms offer services in seller financing. Those that
don't specialize have useful experience with seller financing.
The categories are divided into two distinct types.

Type # 1
There are one-time providers that usually offer their services on
or before the close of escrow.

Type # 2
There are ongoing providers that monitor, maintain and enforce
your agreement throughout its term.

Type 1: One-Time Providers ---------

Promissory Note Buyers

AmeriFunds - 855-853-0759
http://amerifunds.us

Armstrong Capital – 800-845-3055
www.armstrongcapital.com

Note Professionals – 888-563-3918
www.noteprofessionals.com

Seller Assistance Finding Buyers

GGB Capital – 415-400-4077
www.ggbcapital.com

Real Estate Attorneys

Listing all appropriate attorneys in the U.S. would be inefficient, even if all attorneys in America were listed on this book's website, so search local attorneys by accessing "Real Estate Law" on the website http://lawyers.findlaw.com

211

Title Companies
In order by market share

First American Title Insurance
800-854-3643
http://www.firstam.com/title/find-an-office/index.html

Old Republic National Title
800-328-4441
http://www.oldrepublictitle.com/locations/

Chicago Title insurance Company
877-477-2880
http://www.ctic.com/
Input only your city and state

Fidelity National Title Insurance
888-934-3354
http://www.fntic.com/Office.aspx
Input only your city and state

Stewart Title Guaranty Company

800-729-1900
http://www.stewart.com/en/locate-an-issuing-office.html

Escrow Companies

There are far fewer escrow firms than title companies and escrow firms are not nationwide.

New Venture (San Diego CA)
619-327-2288
http://newventureescrow.com

Open Escrow – (Dallas TX)
214-520-9800
http://openescrow.com

SMPR Title & Escrow (Albany NY)
518-434-0127
http://smprtitle.com

Home Inspectors

There are more independent inspectors in every area of the country than either title or escrow firms. Be careful to check for online reviews.

Three best known are AmeriSpec, US Inspect and USA Home Inspections. Check your area for local service.

www.amerispec.com   877-769-5217
www.usinspect.com   888-874-6773
www.usahomeinspections.com 800-491-5030

Type 2: Ongoing Providers -----------

Promissory Note Servicers

There are many responsibilities associated with monitoring "the Note." The most basic involves sending out a monthly account statement to both the buyer and the seller. There are many aspects needing attention on a daily, monthly and annual basis.

As an example, many owner finance sellers don't realize they are supposed to send an IRS Form 1099 to their borrower at the end of each year. The 1099 allows the borrower to claim a deduction for mortgage interest paid. Creating a 1099 INT is just one of many functions that a Note servicer provides.

Servicers usually send the three credit bureaus notice of payment or non-payment on a monthly basis. This keeps both parties honest. The seller is supposed to be paying the existing loans every month and the buyer is obligated to pay the seller.

As you will see in "What to Expect" below, monthly pricing for these valuable services is higher for non-performing Notes. In general, the pricing includes both old and new government required paperwork associated with the seller finance.

Elements of Servicing the Promissory Note
- Generally What to Expect

Step 1 – Servicer Validates the Note

The Note will be accepted for service only if it contains the following items and they are complete and accurate:

Appendix C – Third Party Services

1. Initial Balance of the Note and the Funding Date

2. How Collateral Docs are Transferred and When

3. Servicing Requirements and Info

4. Sellers Representations and Warrants

5. Buyers Reps and Warrants

6. Governing Laws (in case of dispute)

Exhibit showing asset location, sales price, unpaid principal balance, interest rate and lien position

The items above do not necessarily indicate the Note's value.

Step 2 - Wire the Funds to Servicer

If no ACH debit had been set up, the buyer must wire funds within 24 hours of the due date. If a 10% down had been arranged and paid, the buyer gets 5 days to wire the payment.

Be aware that these terms do not apply to all Note servicers

Step 3 – Servicer Receives Proof of Collateral

Original Note
Original Deed of Trust or Mortgage

Original Executed and Notarized Assignment from Seller to Buyer

215

Step 4 A - Setup Standard Servicing

Performing Notes – General Pricing
(see Appendix B for definition of Performing Notes)

Cost $15 - $25/mo. (no impound account)

Cost $30 - $40/mo. (with impound account)

Step 4 B – Setup Specialty Loan Servicing

Non Performing Notes – General Pricing
(see Appendix B – definition of Non Performing Notes)

Cost $35 to $100 per month
Includes sending out RESPA Letters

The sample Note Servicing Form on the following page is associated with NSC (Note Servicing Center).

A sample account servicing agreement from Evergreen Note Servicing follows the NSC Note Servicing Form.

Appendix C – Third Party Services

Note Servicing Center (NSC)
sellerloans.com
3275 E. Robertson Blvd, Suite B
Chowchilla, CA 93610
559-665-3456

Note Servicing Center, Inc.

3275 E. Robertson Blvd., Suite B Chowchilla, CA 93610 ♦ 559-665-3456 ♦ Fax 559-665-3457
info@sellerloans.com ♦ www.sellerloans.com ♦ DRE Corp License No: 01488159

Note Information Form

Lender Information
**Attach Additional Lender Addendum if Loan is Multi-Lender

Name*				
Address*				
City		State	Zip Code	
Home		Work		
Mobil		Fax		
Email				

Borrower
**Attach Additional Borrower Addendum if Loan has more then one Borrower

Name*				
Address*				
City		State	Zip Code	
Home		Work		
Mobil		Fax		
Email				

Note Terms

General		Loan Balances	
Original Balance*		Current Balance*	
Unearned Discount		Unpaid Late Charges	
Note Interest Rate*		Unpaid Charges**	
Sold Rate		Unpaid Interest	
Priority			

Important Dates		Payment Frequency	
Funding*		Payment Frequency*	
Closing*		Day Due*	
First Payment*		Regular Payment	
Purchase		Monthly P&I Payment*	
Interest Paid To*		Total Underlying Payment **	
Next Payment*		Total Escrow Payment**	
Next Revision		Total Monthly Payment	
Maturity*			

* Critical for Servicing
**Additional Addendums Needed

Buy a House with No Bank Loan   Dean Harris

Appendix C – Third Party Services

Evergreen Note Servicing
notecollection.com
208 N Meridian
Puyallup, WA 98371
(253) 848-5678

Account Servicing Agreement

Evergreen Note Servicing (hereinafter referred to as "Servicer"), is hereby directed to establish a servicing account on behalf of the below named parties.

Evergreen Account Number: _____

Seller/Payee:

Last Name (Company)	First Name	SSN	Disbursement %

Last Name	First Name	SSN	

Mailing Address		City	State	Zip

Phone Number(s)	Email Address	Email Receipts? Yes ☐ No ☐

Purchaser/Payor:

Last Name (Company)	First Name	SSN

Last Name	First Name	SSN

Mailing Address		City	State	Zip

Phone Number(s)	Email Address	Email Receipts? Yes ☐ No ☐

Property Address

☐ Primary Residence
☐ Secondary Residence
☐ Investment Property

Site Address _____
Tax Parcel Number(s): _____   Property Type: _____

Documents Deposited	Original	Copy
Promissory Note	☐	☐
Deed of Trust	☐	☐
Signed Request for Reconveyance	☐	☐
Real Estate Contract	☐	☐
Fulfillment Deed	☐	☐
Other: _____	☐	☐

Account Services Fee Agreement	Payor	Seller	Split
Setup Fee*	☐	☐	☐
Monthly Fee*	☐	☐	☐
Optional Services Fee Agreement			
Impound Fee	☐	☐	☐
Prior Lien/Underlying Fee	☐	☐	☐
Late Notice Service Fee	☐	☐	☐

☐ Copy Late Notice to Payee (for additional fee)

Loan Purpose
Purchase ☐   Refinance ☐   Rental/Lease ☐

Mailed Payment Advices	☐	☐	*Required

(fee for mailed advices; no charge for email)

Total Fee (Servicer Completes) _____

Payee fees will be deducted from payment proceeds. Payor fees will be added to the payment amount and collected with each payment. Delinquent Payor fees may be collected from subsequent payments received. All fees and charges are subject to change with thirty (30) days' written notice to parties. Parties agree to pay additional fees charges for extraordinary services, including, but not limited to whenever (a) Servicer renders additional services not set forth herein, (b) conditions of this collection are not promptly fulfilled, (c) manual interest calculations or disbursements must be made because of changes therein or in underlying reserves, or (d) parties become involved in litigation concerning this Agreement or the documents.

218

Buy a House with No Bank Loan   Dean Harris

Homeowner's Insurance Companies

Whether or not you paid for the house entirely in cash, the house may need to be repaired or replaced. It doesn't matter if you owe the bank or the seller. Your debt will still need to be paid in full - even if the house burns to the ground.

Homeowner's insurance will send a check to cover expensive damages or even a total loss - minus the deductible.

The cost of insurance is usually under $1,000 per year. Based on the value the policy provides, the premiums are cheap.

Notice when you are online that nationwide sales phone numbers are no longer provided. Your browser should automatically sense your location, or you may need to input your zip code.

State Farm
www.statefarm.com/insurance/home-and-property/homeowners

Allstate
www.allstate.com/home-insurance/homeowners-insurance-basics.aspx

Farmers
www.farmers.com/home/homeowners/

Liberty Mutual
www.libertymutual.com/homeowners-insurance

Home Warranty Firms

There are more firms than ever to protect appliances, plumbing, electrical, roof, etc. Not all providers will cover all items in all categories. Call or visit their websites to find out exactly what is and is not covered.

These firms do not compete with homeowner's insurance firms. Unlike warranties, homeowner's insurance is usually required by the lending institution and does not generally cover common smaller incidents that are covered by the warranty firms.

Homeowner's insurance sends the homeowner a check minus the deductible. Homeowner's insurance almost never sends out service technicians to do repairs as warranty firms do.

Based on the ever skyrocketing cost of plumbing or electrical incidents, these two categories alone will pay for the annual home warranty premium and service visit.

Be careful to also compare each warranty firm's visit charge. Most are between $50 and $80. That service visit (or service call) is an additional charge for each incident you report. The service call is an out-of-pocket expense that is not included in the policy's monthly or annual premium. Premiums range $250 to $500 a year, with a typical cost of about $350.

Keep in mind that these covered charges are much smaller than most service and labor charges that are not covered. As another caution, be sure to read the fine print so you have a better idea what the home warranty firm will and will not cover.

Home Warranty Firms (continued)

- ## American Home Shield
  Many consider this the best provider, possibly because of its longevity. It was one of the first warranty providers.
  www.ahs.com 888-429-8247

- ## First American Home Warranty
  This is another popular service. Compare this firm with American Home Shield to begin your evaluation.
  www.fahw.com 888-650-2895

- ## Choice Home Warranty
  www.choicehomewarranty.com 888-531-5403

- ## EquityLock Protector
  EquityLock primarily offers equity protection. Their home warranty offerings are separate from their equity product.
  http://equitylocksolutions.com 800-401-9290

- ## TotalProtect
  www.totalprotect.com 866-607-9674

- ## Select Home Warranty
  https://selecthomewarranty.com 855-267-3532

- ## Old Republic Home Protection
  www.orhp.com 800-445-6999

Appendix D – Mortgage vs Trust Deed

In the U.S. certain states are known as "judicial" states and others are known as "non-judicial" states.

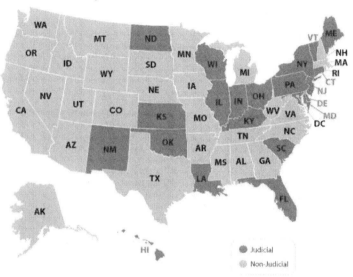

Figure 9 – Mortgage versus Trust Deed States

As you can see, there are fewer judicial states than non-judicial states. Judicial states, also known as "mortgage states," still depend on the court system to handle foreclosure.

It wasn't so long ago that non-judicial, or "trust deed" states, were in the minority.

Keep in mind that some non-judicial states have areas within them that are judicial, and vice versa. Even those areas are

222

rapidly becoming a non-judicial majority, indicating the possible extinction of mortgages altogether.

The recent epidemic of foreclosures put additional time pressures on the already burdened court systems to perform. In fact, the volume has proven to be overwhelming.

Many judicial states and areas around them are in the process of converting to the non-judicial system in order to avoid future excessive costs and delays.

Deficiency

Notice that the last column in Figure 10 mentions this term. What exactly does "deficiency" mean in this context?

Many of the states that allow lenders to seek deficiencies limit the amount that lenders can recover.

In residential housing, the deficiency is the difference between the outstanding loan amount and the fair market value of the house

As an example, the amount owed on a loan is $350,000, the house is sold in a foreclosure sale for $150,000, and the fair market value of the house is $200,000.

A deficiency lawsuit would limit the lender's recovery to $150,000 ($350,000 minus $200,000), although the deficiency was actually $200,000 (which was $350,000 minus $150,000).

Appendix D – Mortgage vs Trust Deed

State	Security Instrument	Foreclosure Type	Initial Step	# of Months	Redemption	Deficiency
Alabama	Mortgage	Nonjudicial	Publication	1	12 months	Allowed
Alaska	Trust Deed	Nonjudicial	Notice of Default	3	None	Allowed
Arizona	Trust Deed	Nonjudicial	Notice of Sale	3	None	Allowed
Arkansas	Mortgage	Judicial	Complaint	4	None	Allowed
California	Trust Deed	Nonjudicial	Notice of Default	4	None	Prohibited
Colorado	Trust Deed	Nonjudicial	Notice of Default	2	75 Days	Allowed
Connecticut	Mortgage	Strict	Complaint	5	None	Allowed
Delaware	Mortgage	Judicial	Complaint	3	None	Allowed
Dist. of Col.	Trust Deed	Nonjudicial	Notice of Default	2	None	Allowed
Florida	Mortgage	Judicial	Complaint	5	None	Allowed
Georgia	Security Deed	Nonjudicial	Publication	2	None	Allowed
Hawaii	Mortgage	Nonjudicial	Publication	3	None	Allowed
Idaho	Trust Deed	Nonjudicial	Notice of Default	5	None	Allowed
Illinois	Mortgage	Judicial	Complaint	7	None	Allowed
Indiana	Mortgage	Judicial	Complaint	5	3 months	Allowed
Iowa	Mortgage	Judicial	Petition	5	6 months	Allowed
Kansas	Mortgage	Judicial	Complaint	4	6–12 months	Allowed
Kentucky	Mortgage	Judicial	Complaint	6	None	Allowed
Louisiana	Mortgage	Exec. Process	Petition	2	None	Allowed
Maine	Mortgage	Judicial	Complaint	6	None	Allowed
Maryland	Trust Deed	Nonjudicial	Notice	2	None	Allowed
Massachusetts	Mortgage	Judicial	Complaint	3	None	Allowed
Michigan	Mortgage	Nonjudicial	Publication	2	6 months	Allowed
Minnesota	Mortgage	Nonjudicial	Publication	2	6 months	Prohibited
Mississippi	Trust Deed	Nonjudicial	Publication	2	None	Prohibited
Missouri	Trust Deed	Nonjudicial	Publication	2	None	Allowed
Montana	Trust Deed	Nonjudicial	Notice	5	None	Prohibited
Nebraska	Mortgage	Judicial	Petition	5	None	Allowed
Nevada	Trust Deed	Nonjudicial	Notice of Default	4	None	Allowed

Figure 10 – Mortgage vs. Trust Deed States - (chart continues)

Buy a House with No Bank Loan   Dean Harris

Appendix D – Mortgage vs Trust Deed

State	Security Instrument	Foreclosure Type	Initial Step	# of Months	Redemption	Deficiency
New Hampshire	Mortgage	Nonjudicial	Notice of Sale	2	None	Allowed
New Jersey	Mortgage	Judicial	Complaint	3	10 Days	Allowed
New Mexico	Mortgage	Judicial	Complaint	4	None	Allowed
New York	Mortgage	Judicial	Complaint	4	None	Allowed
North Carolina	Trust Deed	Nonjudicial	Notice Hearing	2	None	Allowed
North Dakota	Mortgage	Judicial	Complaint	3	60 Days	Prohibited
Ohio	Mortgage	Judicial	Complaint	5	None	Allowed
Oklahoma	Mortgage	Judicial	Complaint	4	None	Allowed
Oregon	Trust Deed	Nonjudicial	Notice of Default	5	None	Allowed
Pennsylvania	Mortgage	Judicial	Complaint	3	None	Allowed
Rhode Island	Mortgage	Nonjudicial	Publication	2	None	Allowed
South Carolina	Mortgage	Judicial	Complaint	6	None	Allowed
South Dakota	Mortgage	Judicial	Complaint	3	180 days	Allowed
Tennessee	Trust Deed	Nonjudicial	Publication	2	None	Allowed
Texas	Trust Deed	Nonjudicial	Publication	2	None	Allowed
Utah	Trust Deed	Nonjudicial	Notice of Default	4	None	Allowed
Vermont	Mortgage	Judicial	Complaint	7	None	Allowed
Virginia	Trust Deed	Nonjudicial	Publication	2	None	Allowed
Washington	Trust Deed	Nonjudicial	Notice of Default	4	None	Allowed
West Virginia	Trust Deed	Nonjudicial	Publication	2	None	Prohibited
Wisconsin	Mortgage	Judicial	Complaint	Varies	None	Allowed
Wyoming	Mortgage	Nonjudicial	Publication	2	3 months	Allowed

Figure 10 – Mortgage versus Trust Deed States (continued)

225

Buy a House with No Bank Loan   Dean Harris

Index

Debt to Income Ratio (DTI)

Dodd-Frank

Federal Reserve Bank

foreclosure

former U.S. Presidents

Index

Made in the USA
Middletown, DE
11 August 2018